Contents

DR. MASAAKI HATSUMI

ESSENCE
OF
NINJUTSU

The Nine Traditions

CONTEMPORARY BOOKS

Library of Congress Cataloging-in-Publication Data

Hatsumi, Masaaki, 1931–
  Essence of ninjutsu.
   p. cm.
  Includes index.
  ISBN 0-8092-4724-0
  1. Ninjutsu—History. I. Title.
UB271.J3H328 1988
 796.8'6—dc21   88-30190
             CIP

Published by Contemporary Books
A division of NTC/Contemporary Publishing Group, Inc.
4255 West Touhy Avenue, Lincolnwood (Chicago), Illinois 60712-1975 U.S.A.
Copyright © 1988 by Dr. Masaaki Hatsumi
Printed in the United States of America
International Standard Book Number: 0-8092-4724-0

12 13 14 15 16 VRS/VRS 0 8 7 6 5

Introduction
Translating the Space
Between the Lines

In my view, my mother language is unique in that it has virtually kept its own linguistic arena of a single nation and a single society, despite occasional cultural exchanges with other nations.

I presume the translation work of my book on ninjutsu is not an easy task. For Japanese writing, especially kanji or Chinese characters, has many homonyms and I have tried to make the most of this characteristic of my native language in order to make my expressions more vivid. This is what I call a ninja style of writing. This ninja-style writing is a method of displaying my literary talent. In order to give full play to this literary stage, my translator (*honyaku sha* in Japanese) must be also the other leading actor (also *honyaku sha* or *shuyaku* in Japanese). Mr Hirai and I are coactors on the same stage.

Mr. Hirai said to me, "I was not surprised by the thickness of your manuscript, but by the depth of the meaning you tried to incorporate into each word. Frankly speaking I often stopped tapping the keys of my word processor to think out what you wanted to express. I sometimes had to put one word in perspective."

I replied, "I am sorry for using a style that is hard to translate into English. I feel as if I were an irresponsible parent who had begotten a baby and had someone else take care of it. But you understand me very well. I've talked with you as often as possible, because I wanted you to understand me better. We are living in an age where a translating machine is replacing the human brain. I believe a better translation depends upon an individual's linguistic abilities and insight."

Mr. Hirai is a man of thoughtfulness and great insight, to say nothing of his linguistic ability. Our collaboration would often have exchanges like the following:

Mr. Hirai asked, "*Kami* is generally translated into 'god' in English, which is misleading. Besides, there are many religions in the world. What do you mean specifically by kami? You also referred to *shinrei* and *kamurozan* in your book."

I gave him a ready answer: "By *kami* I mean the recognition of universal justice. *Shinrei* is the divine spirit. And *kamurozan* means the closest mountain to the heavenly justice."

I have made great efforts with my body, words, and heart in order to make my ninjutsu, my view of martial arts, and myself understood by the people of the world. However, it seems to me that instead of kamurozan there stands a mountain of desires in many people's way: whenever I call out, my voice echoes back without reaching the ears of the people. But since kamurozan is transparent, the people beyond the mountain could hear my voice without difficulty if they listened.

I recollect a certain scholar to have said that what one has to keep in mind when meeting foreigners is to try to understand how differently things are conceived in foreign languages from the way they are in Japanese. This holds true of translating Japanese into a foreign language. The mere translation of one word into another in a different language is no good. Thus, I understand how difficult and important translation work is and that it needs deep understanding of the background of the language into which one wants to translate. If I happen to be thrown into the world of a foreign language, I might be confused into thinking that the color TV I am watching has been abruptly replaced with a black and white one or the three-dimensional TV with an ordinary one—so great is the difference between one's mother tongue and a foreign one.

The difficulty in translation from one language into another or communication across different languages in general can be compared to that of an international marriage. Since it is a marriage, the man and woman should enjoy a considerable, if not complete, degree of understanding in the name of love. Nevertheless, the couple's communication

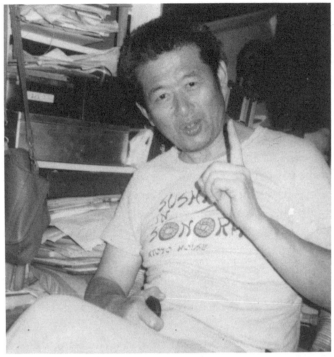

The author, Dr. Masaaki Hatsumi.

The translator, Mr. Masaru Hirai.

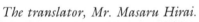

or translation is far from perfect. This is not only because of their language problem but because of their comprehension of how and what their partner thinks.

This is true of the relationship between teacher and student or between friends. While one tries to do one's utmost to make oneself understood, the other, despite some self-confidence that he understands you well, sometimes breaks the bond of friendship or the relationship because of his biased way of understanding or translation. Many students of mine live in various parts of the world. They have their own native languages and their own way of thinking. Trapped in their way of thinking, they could be poor communicators or translators, unable to touch the most important thing. To avoid this, an untiring search for true translation on the part of each individual is needed. This is what Mr. Hirai and I accomplished. Mr. Harai said to me, "I don't think there can be a good translation without deep understanding of the background of the text. In the case of your book, I had to pay much attention to over one thousand years of Japanese culture."

A Japanese scholar named Inazo Nitobe translated the book *Bushido or the Way of the Samurai* into English and published it in the United States. I hear it was widely read, but I wonder how many people could understand the spirit of the samurai. The reason I raise this question is that I hear Mr. Nitobe himself has said that what matters in a book is read between the lines or in the spaces between the words. I hope his words will make Mr. Hirai feel a little relaxed because the same is the case with my book. If my readers find the book rather difficult, please try to read between the lines where you can feel a breath of the sustained life of the ninjutsu handed down from a thousand years ago.

Incidentally, Mr. Charles S. Terry, a friend of mine, is a translator of the book *Miyamoto Musashi* by Eiji Yoshikawa. His translation was wonderful enough to have been a bestseller in the United States. In Japan many authors have written about Miyamoto Musashi. History makes a variety of images of the same person. Several images of the single person are created by many writers. It seems to me that this is also a kind of translation. Then, it follows that the translation is not limited to the work of expression in another language.

The translator of this book is Mr. Masaru Harai. My other two books were translated into English by Mr. and Mrs. Stephen K. Hayes and Mr. Chris W. P. Reynolds. Perhaps my readers wonder why I asked three persons to translate my books. My intention is to make myself better understood by all of you, my readers. This is a sanshin no kata or tricenter technique, one of the secrets of taijutsu. A single mind may lead one to a wrong judgment. In contrast, an attempt at enlightenment with three minds will be one of the surest ways of attaining it.

This is what I often tell my students. It is natural that each translator should have his own way of interpretation and style. Yet through their eyes, hearts, and subjective interpretation you will be able to penetrate from three different aspects my views on ninjutsu or martial arts—how I have gone through the training—and my way of thinking.

Contemporary Books, Inc., has published three books of mine and I deeply appreciate the kindness of my editor Mr. Donavan Vicha. I also thank all the translators of my books for their painstaking efforts. *Time*, *effort*, and *gratitude* are the three words that come into my mind the moment I begin to think about the difficulty my translators may have had.

An ascetic.

Tsujigiri

Long ago, there were brazen fighters who tested their ability by committing tsujigiri (testing one's sword on live, innocent victims). This is a story from when Takamatsu sensei was 18 years of age. In his father's factory they needed about 330 gallons of clear water a day. Every morning, using a pole and four brackets, Jutaro brought all of the water to the factory. This was a feat that no one else could perform. The water came from the mouth of a stone turtle, which consistently gave out clear water. This turtle was located a little way down from Maruyama mountain, which was seven to eight blocks away from the factory. Each load weighed 529 pounds and a total of five trips from the turtle were needed. Jutaro said that this was perfect for conditioning his legs and waist.

One day a factory worker said, "Young master, I had a hell of a time last night. I was working alone on Shin bashi bridge when a man blocked my way. If I moved to the right to pass him, he moved to block me and did the same if I moved to the left. Then, he grabbed me by my collar and threw me into the water. I thought I was going to be killed. Young master, I don't really want to go on errands in that area after dark." Overhearing this conversation, another worker added, "Really? Me, too. Isn't this like the tsujigiris of olden times?"

Hearing this, Jutaro said, "Leave it to me."

Shin bashi bridge is at the point where the river enters from the Akashi seashore. The sailors tie their small boats to the banks here and leave for the sea from this spot. On the shores there are seventeen or eighteen whorehouses. That night Jutaro crossed Shin bashi bridge four or five times without anything happening. The next day he did the same with the same result. Jutaro said to himself, "Maybe this ruffian is someone who knows me."

The following night he wore a disguise and went to the bridge. As expected, when he was halfway across the bridge, a man wearing a hat to cover his eyes came walking toward him. Jutaro moved to the left to pass him but the fellow moved in his way. The same thing happened when he moved to the right. Then he grabbed Jutaro by the collar and tried to throw him by using his hip. Jutaro stuck out his stomach and let his arms down loosely. The man persistently tried to throw him; then tried to hit Jutaro with his fist, then tried to kick him. But all his punches and kicks hit air. When the man became confused, Jutaro threw him upside down, yelling a kiai. The man's hat flew away and he fell down on his stomach, stretched out like a dead spider. Jutaro turned the man over to see his face and to apply the art of resuscitation. It was one of Mizuta sensei's students, Miyata, who held a middle rank license in jujutsu. Jutaro angrily lectured him. "How could you disgrace your school in this way? You should be ashamed!"

1
Yamagomori and Shutsuzan

Everyone is familiar with the story that Yoshitsune of the Minamoto family, called Ushiwakamaru in his younger days, had studied martial arts under Kiichihogen at Mount Kurama, where a warrior god named Bishamonten is enshrined. People have different motivations for secluding themselves in the mountains to study ninpo or other martial arts. In the case of my mentor, Takagi Oriemon, from whom I took over the Takagi ryu, his motive for spending thirty-seven days in training at Mount Kurama was his desire to understand why he lost in a match against Yagyu Tajimano-kami of the Yagyu ryu.

Oreimon had a dream on the day he fulfilled his vow of thirty-seven days of continuous training. In the dream, he was being attacked by a large, fierce tiger and the tiger became bigger and bigger as it came closer to him. Oriemon tried to aim his spear right at the tiger's face. Suddenly a dark, black cloud appeared and the dream seemed to fade away.

The faint sound of chanting descended from the clouds and drifted about like the sound that hangs in the air of the pitch-black world of dreams. The clouds dispersed and a full moon shone. At that moment Oriemon intuitively realized the importance of one's eyes. Oriemon had

Bishamonten (drawing by Takamatsu sensei).

a rematch with Yagyu, and records show that he took up his sword, aimed for Yagyu's eyes, and was victorious.

Some of you may doubt that this was a dream. But a dream can be understood as a way to express a spiritual awakening concerning the intersection of the void and present reality: a large tiger can be likened to an extremely strong warrior; and true darkness can represent how one's mind and body drift in space.

I realize that such explanations are hard to understand. The only thing that can be said is that we abide by the rules of expression of the martial arts. This means making use of forms of magical expression and rhythmical music to communicate the essence of the art. There is a saying: "The village that shines in the moonlight leaves a different impression in the souls of different people." The Chinese characters for strength and nothingness are both read *mu* in Japanese. Therefore, nothingness is the same as strength. I hope you understand that my intention is to introduce you to the world of ninpo through the method of expression based on nothingness. Do not, however, confuse the essence of satori (enlightenment) and kaigen (spiritual awakening). Let us attempt to glimpse the essence of initiation into the mysteries of ninjutsu by following the experience of Takamatsu sensei as he gained spiritual insight into ninjutsu and budo or the ways of the warrior.

Takamatsu sensei's name as a child was Jutaro. Jutaro, in March of the twenty-third year of his life, came home to Japan. In his heart he longed to visit the grave of his girlfriend Kogane, and also to visit his grandmother. She lived in the Higashi Shirikecho district of Hyogo city. When she saw his face, she cried with joy. He told her the reason for his return to Japan. Unfortunately, he did not return to share success but had come home to cure his illness, beriberi. He implied that he wanted to use her house to recover. She opened her house to him and told him to rest without caring for anything besides recovering.

A month had passed when a messenger from his father in Akashi arrived. He said that if the grandmother insisted on caring for the young Jutaro, the father would stop sending her a monthly allowance. The grandmother replied, "Who would take care of my darling grandson in his illness if I do not? His father tells me I cannot take care of him—that he will stop sending my allowance. Let him stop sending his money! I will take care of my grandson if I have to work in my old age to do it. Please relate what I have said to my son."

While she was sending the messenger away Jutaro crawled out of his sickbed and told the messenger, "Thank goodness you have come! I was planning to leave soon. I will be well enough in a couple of days."

His grandmother knew that he was not only afflicted with beriberi but his lungs were also damaged, so she said with tears streaming down her face, "Jutaro, never mind what your father says, I will cure your illness no matter what I have to do. You stay here and rest."

Jutaro would not allow himself to cause her any inconvenience on his behalf. Even if it killed him, he could not go against the way of the ninja. He remembered the smiling face of his master, Toda sensei, saying "Even when you are faced with certain death, die laughing."

Two days after the messenger had come, he decided to leave. He thought the sooner he left, the less the inconvenience he would cause his grandmother. He waited for her to go out of the house and then left without anything but the clothes he happened to be wearing. He decided his destination was to be Mayasan mountain. (Maya is the mother of Buddha.) Dragging his heavy legs afflicted with beriberi and swollen to the size of an elephant's, Takamatsu sensei journeyed towards Kamenotaki falls of the mountain to see his "natural" mother, whom he had not met yet. If he had not trained in ninjutsu, the state of his legs would have made it impossible to move. The sense of justice he had, what made him so badly want to live without inconveniencing his grandmother, forced his legs to move.

It was early summer. Jutaro looked up to heaven as he climbed the mountain path. Sometimes his eyes were filled with tears as he made the great effort to take each step. "Kogane also died! I'm going to die anyway, so I prefer to die in solitude."

It was still the rainy season, but the sun was very strong. As a child, Jutaro had climbed Mt. Maya many times but it seemed to take forever to climb the mountain that day; it seemed higher than usual. He crawled on his hands and knees, but finally reached Kamenotaki (Turtle Falls).

He arrived at a small hut. It was only about two tatami mats in size or about four meters square. The hut had board walls about two meters high and was quite airy. He had purchased three sho (about half a gallon) of unpolished rice at a rice store at the foot of the mountain. The rice had been so heavy that it seemed as if he had carried an entire bale of rice up the mountain.

Jutaro did not bring any matches because he didn't smoke. The moment he thought, "Damn, I forgot to bring matches," he recalled what his master had taught him. Toda sensei had said, "It is important for a ninja to eat uncooked food; one should not take food that is cooked. People begin losing stamina and energy and their sixth sense as a result of eating cooked food."

At that moment, Jutaro's soul was touched by the light of his master's teachings. Toda sensei had said, "Ninja must become familiar with eating natural food. We can also eat food without cooking it. First, we need water. But drinking water is not enough. You can fill your chest with fresh mountain air." Jutaro forced a laugh as he began to understand why people say hermits live on air.

Jutaro washed the rice and laid it out on a stone. He used the sun's rays like an oven, and soon the rice became powdery after rubbing it between his palms. You can pop such rice into your mouth and grind it with your teeth. (Typical ninja dishes also make use of nuts, roots, and mountain grasses.) Jutaro talked to a photograph of Toda sensei as he ate. A light appeared before the food. He continued to eat as he thought about Toda sensei, Ishitani sensei, and Mizutani sensei, who were in heaven, and the raw rice began to taste like the most delicious food in the world.

Jutaro felt that he regained some stamina. Solitude makes a person's heart cold so he decided to find some friends. The wind and birds called to him. Animals called to him from a distance.

It was inconvenient to move along the trail in the evening as there were no lights, but Jutaro had no difficulty because he had mastered the ninpo technique of seeing through the darkness.

One evening, Jutaro was suddenly awakened when someone shouted, "Kaire!" (Go home!). The earsplitting shout reached his gut and interrupted the dark stillness of the night. Jutaro was brave, however, and went back to sleep. He later found out that it was a half-awake bird.

One day at dawn, Jutaro heard the sounds of people walking along the edge of the falls. They were enjoying a bath under the falls and chanting prayers. Perhaps they were training in the teachings of the Buddha because Jutaro could also hear their voices reciting Buddhist scriptures in the distance. He did not know anything about prayers or scriptures. He was just totally exhausted, so he lay down with his body and soul wrapped in a simple kimono.

Although it was June, it got quite cold in the evenings and the cold mountain air attacked the body. To fight the cold, Jutaro crawled along with his arms, dragging his lifeless legs behind him. Perhaps the spirit of the full moon reflected in the water lured him to enter the falls. Jutaro seemed to float in the pool and let the water from the falls hit his body. He began to repeat the prayers that the followers had been chanting and to recite scriptures that he had never learned as if the waterfall had stimulated his vocal chords.

Several days later, an old man saw Jutaro bathing under the falls and came to speak to him. "Young man. You seem to be practicing asceticism, but what are you praying for?"

Jutaro could barely speak but he replied, "I want to cure my illness."

The old man's eyes gave off a warm light. "That should not be such a difficult task. You've got beriberi, and you have tapeworms in your stomach. I can cure you. Let's get rid of the tapeworms first." He folded his hands into one of the kuji-in hand positions—to-in (sword seals)—and with a yell, he stabbed Jutaro in the stomach with it and then murmured to himself.

Jutaro wondered with some degree of suspicion, "How can this old man think that he can cure tapeworms in such a superstitious fashion?"

The old man said, "You'll be rid of the tapeworms in two or three

Ninja sitting on a stone in training (drawing by author).

days. I'll be back, my young friend." He climbed a rock and walked away but it seemed as if his feet did not touch the ground.

The rain let up and the sun began to shine on the third day after the old man left. Jutaro felt an extreme pain in his stomach and ran behind the hut to relieve himself. He found two different-looking tapeworms. Upon careful examination, he saw that one tapeworm had a vertical line down its back while the other had a horizontal stripe.

"How strange, indeed!

"He really did it. What a strange old man!" Jutaro began to feel attracted by the old man's mysterious power.

About ten days later, the old man appeared again. "How are you, young man? I believe you have gotten rid of the tapeworms."

"Yes. Let me thank you very much." Jutaro dragged his heavy feet to get closer to the old man.

The old man who had been watching with penetrating eyes said, "Good. Then we'll take care of the beriberi today." The old man folded his hands into the to-in hand position again. "And this time, it won't take ten days to fully cure you, so don't worry."

When he was done, the old man disappeared again without making a sound.

Without realizing it, Jutaro became preoccupied with this strange old man. He also began to recover his senses.

On the morning of the seventh day, Jutaro vowed that he would sit under the falls and that he would stand. He crawled under the waterfall with the help of a rock. A large amount of water came crashing down on Jutaro, pushing his body and shoulders down, but his legs were able to withstand the weight. Jutaro was filled with delight. "I'm alive!" He felt as if he could climb the waterfall by pushing aside the water.

After climbing on top of the rock, Jutaro once again tested his body. He leaped from one rock to another, as if he had grown a pair of wings. He made up his mind to begin by practicing Koto and Togakure ryu exercises and waited for the next morning.

Awake before the break of day, Jutaro was practising taijutsu on the rock and was so full of vitality that it seemed as if he were kicking with the energy of the sun. With the light against his back he kicked a rock and shattered it. He climbed a large tree, did a somersault, and jumped back to the ground again. He practiced flying kicks in the water.

Jutaro went by another name—Kikaku (Demon's Horns) Jutaro—and as this name implies, he was a man who would go through with something once he set his mind to it.

Animals from the neighboring mountains gathered to watch and the strange old man returned as if he could feel the strong spirit with which Jutaro crushed rocks and knocked down high trees regardless of his broken toes. "It looks like you've fully recovered," he said and Jutaro seemed to be enveloped by the old man's compassionate eyes.

"Thank you very much. Thanks to your help, I have fully recovered. You possess a special power. Are you a doctor that visits patients in these mountains?"

"You say odd things. Human beings only see with the eyes on their faces and do not like to use the eyes inside their hearts. You do this. But people say they can't and that's because they don't know how."

"Is that so?"

"You've got a lot of training in martial arts. Your sharp eyesight and movement left an impression on my intuitive eyes."

"You even know that I have been practicing martial arts," replied Jutaro. "I am still a beginner. Toda sensei often said one should not have a glance or attitude that lets others know that one is practicing martial arts."

"I think it's all right because you are so young.

"When I compare the inner truth of martial arts and of religion, I see that they are very similar in nature."

This episode helps me to recall how a conversation unfolded between Takamatsu sensei and myself thirteen years ago. It was about one year before he died. He said, "I have decided to leave everything in the hands of Masaaki Hatsumi. I think you are the most suitable person as far as martial arts are concerned. I am now able to repay Toda sensei and Ishitani sensei for their kindnesses. I intend to continue my studies into the secrets of nature."

"For example," the old man continued, "I can predict that the enemy will come before it actually does. I can even knock down an enemy that I cannot see. I knew beforehand that you would fall ill. You possess a special talent that will allow you to become an expert in any field that

Tengu, or a long-nosed goblin, said to be half man and half crow.

My master trained and became spiritually awakened by training in the great mountains of Mother Nature, but let me say that I attained spiritual enlightenment in the asphalt jungle of the big city.

you choose. But you must always remember to foster a proper mental attitude."

With those words, the old man once again disappeared into the mountains.

One day, an ascetic came to the hut to seek shelter from the rain. It had been raining since morning. The ascetic said he had chances to meet many tengu (long-nosed goblins) because he was always training in the mountains. The rain got worse and the ascetic asked to spend the night because he couldn't go home. Jutaro told him he was welcome, but that he didn't have any linen or blankets to offer. The ascetic said that was fine; sleeping on the ground with tree roots was ideal.

In the meantime, it became windy and the rain poured into the nearby pool with a tremendous sound. The wind began to laugh. A large rock crumbled into pieces and fell to the ground. The landslide reached the shed, which was almost pushed into the pool of the waterfall. With all of this commotion, the ascetic began to shiver with fear. Jutaro wondered what had happened to the confidence he had earlier. His visitor said it would be too dangerous to stay and descended the mountain despite the wind and the rain.

Jutaro forced a smile and then lay down. He could hear the sound of the rocks hitting the shed and at the same time, the sound of splintering paneling. The crack came to a stop about thirty centimeters above his head. He murmured in his sleep that the shed was safe. Once again, there was a large creaking sound.

Jutaro was awakened by the bright rays of the sun. He wanted to see the damage that the typhoon had caused but failed to open the back door to get outside. He went out the front and around the hut to discover a pile of rocks. Jutaro was delighted to see the naturally created protective wall and continued with his practice.

One day he saw the reflection of the old man's face in the water and didn't hesitate to call out "Sensei!"

"You're a fine young man. I have decided to teach you all the skills I possess, starting now."

The old man decided to teach Jutaro the skills to predict how long a person will live, to see in the dark, and to bring freedom to animals. It had taken a whole lifetime for the old man to acquire these skills. He also passed on to Jutaro the way to find out about changes in nature and how to predict unhappy calamities before they occurred.

Jutaro began to see the light when he realized that ninjutsu and the skills of karate and jutaijutsu that he had mastered thus far were life skills—for survival. A smile came across Jutaro's face. "I have been training believing that martial arts provided a technique to overcome the enemy, while ninpo was the art of stealth, the way of invisibility. But when I think about the proper direction of gaining enlightenment or the nature of such arts, it all boils down to learning the laws of nature." Jutaro decided to continue his encounter with Mother Nature for another three months. He spent his days in training both his mind and body. The reason that he chose such a period, is that nine is the strongest of the numbers and ten symbolizes taking a vow to realize some desire.

When ninety days had passed, Jutaro said farewell to the large frog, the large snake, and the mountain spring, and to the rocks, and trees that had befriended him during his stay in the mountains, and then descended the mountain.

My master trained and became spiritually awakened by training in the great mountains of Mother Nature, but let me say that I attained spiritual enlightenment in the asphalt jungle of the big city. Savage beasts called human beings live in today's cities. According to British psychoanalyst Dr. Anthony Stowe,

> We human beings are the most cruel and cold-hearted animals that exist on earth. It is a mistake to think that a normal human being cannot become excessively brutal. We all have a savage instinct within us that makes us kill, torture, and fight in wars.

Today's large cities are full of danger. Cars speed through the city and booby traps called scandals can be found everywhere you go. For every obstacle or peril you find in the wilderness, there is a parallel to be found in any big city.

I guess I can call myself a modern day ninja because I attained spiritual awakening by secluding myself in the jungle of today's modern city.

The Story of Sasuke Sarutobi

Masters of the martial arts, including the ninja, would ordinarily seclude themselves in the mountains for training. This period was considered absolutely essential.

We tend to imagine mountain seclusion as very far from human habitation, but that wasn't necessarily so in the case of the ninja. This secluded place must be where the trainee can live in hiding and still sustain life. If there is a path to his hideout, he will be found easily, but it still must be located near a water supply. Thus, he must find an unfrequented area; preferably near a village. *Yamagomori*, which means mountain seclusion in Japanese, can be also interpreted as *yamagakure*, to live secretly without the danger of being attacked by arrows.

Sasuke Sarutobi, one of the heroes of ninjutsu, was created in Tachikawa literature at the end of the Meiji period. Up until that time, the general image of ninjutsu was related to black arts, witchcraft, magic, hobgoblins, thieves, and assassins. Sasuke was a mischievous boy. Books describe him as an innocent child with a strong sense of justice. In the stories, great importance was placed on humor, with actual combat considered secondary.

13

One day, Sasuke said to himself, "I'm already ten years old. It's no longer practical for me to practice yatto (a form of Kiai-spirit shout) with monkeys and deer. I'll follow my father's advice and seek a master swordsman to train me. I'm going to go to Okunoin in the Torie Pass to ask the gods to provide me with a good master."

When Sasuke arrived at Okunoin, he began playing among clumps of trees rather than practicing yatto. Not satisfied with a stick, Sasuke grappled with a large tree, trying to twist it down. Then, he heard someone laughing at him. Sasuke called, "Hey, who are you? I'm concentrating on fencing. Don't you dare laugh at me. Come out here. I'll not forgive you." As he looked around, he saw an old man with swept-back long hair tied at the back of his head smiling at him. The man's hair was as white as snow. Sasuke asked, "Oh, you laughed at me, didn't you, old man?"

The old man answered, "Yes I did."

Sasuke asked him again fiercely, "Why did you laugh at me? Answer me. If there is no good reason, I'll never forgive you even if you are an old man."

The old man laughed and said, "Well, Sasuke, you were practicing with a tree, but this is like practicing with a dead enemy. You can't improve your fencing that way. Do you want to learn fencing so badly?"

This was the age of civil wars, and only a few people could live to an old age. Therefore, Sasuke reasoned, an elderly fencing instructor was surely a master at martial arts.

Sasuke said, "Old man, are you a master of martial arts? I want to learn the secrets of martial arts."

"What are you going to do with them, after you learn them?"

"I'll be a strong swordsman and win fame and honor."

"Wonderful. What an admirable goal for only a boy! All right. I'm going to give you a lesson in consideration of your zeal and determination."

Sasuke prostrated himself before the old man and thanked him. Then, Saskue delivered a sword stroke to the old man. However, he had disappeared. Sasuke looked around nervously. Then, he was suddenly tripped by an attack from behind and fell flat on his face. The old man appeared suddenly in front of Sasuke with a smile.

The old man taught Sasuke for the next three years. He tried to teach him the godan or fifth-level secrets by saying, "Don't you have your eyes in your back? How handicapped you are!

"You'll be a failure unless you know how to defend your weak point, even if you know the unguarded point of your opponent. The secret of defense in martial arts is to always be alert.

"Unless one knows his own weak point, he can never be certain that the weak point of his opponent is not a decoy."

In addition to ankokutoshijutsu techniques for seeing in the dark, Sasuke learned to listen for stealthy footsteps coming from more than thirty meters away.

One day the old man handed a scroll to Sasuke and said to him, "Well, Sasuke, this is my parting gift, the rules of ninjutsu. Carry it with you for life and behave prudently. When you are in combat with others or meet heroes and great men, you'll never be beaten if you understand what is written in this scroll."

When the old man gave the scroll to Sasuke, he for the first time revealed his name as Hakuunsai Tozawa, and then disappeared.

My scroll is a present from Takamatsu sensei. As time went by, I could better understand its secrets. Five, ten, and thirty years have passed since I first read the scroll, and now I can finally see the great meanings hidden within it. In other words, I have found the endless secrets that lie between the lines. If anyone should steal the scroll, it would be useless, because I'm the only one with the experience and enlightenment to read and understand it.

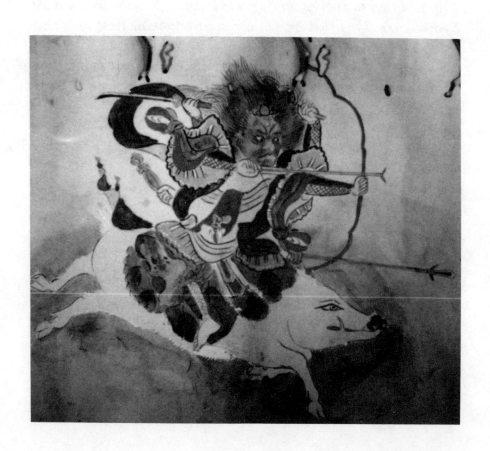

2
A Talk with Takamatsu Sensei

It was one evening in the early fall when "bell-ring" insects sang in the wind, I had an opportunity to speak with Takamatsu sensei about the world of ninjutsu. The following is our conversation:

Hatsumi: Much has been discussed about the origin of ninjutsu. Could you tell me something about it?

Takamatsu: That is hard to answer. After all, I was not born in the era when ninja were taking active roles.

H: Yes, I understand.

T: By the way, as you know, I was taught ninjutsu by my uncle, who used to belong to the samurai class in Iga Province (within present-day Mie Prefecture). He told me many things and had me copy his own writings. But what was more important was that we talked to each other through body and mind.

H: I see. It seems to me that we cannot understand the essence of ninjutsu without talking through body and mind.

T: That's true. Both Toda sensei and Ishitani sensei talked about their own teachers, too. They talked about ninjutsu in olden times, of course—adding some episodes to it. In addition to what my teachers told me, I have read many old books written by the ninja of long ago,

Author, suffering from illness, chats with Takamatsu sensei.

Takamatsu sensei.

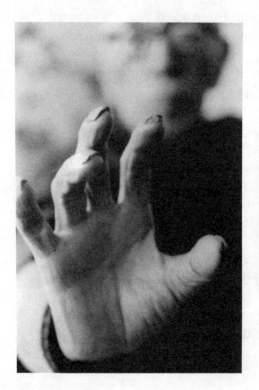

Due to a number of factors in his extraordinary life, Takamatsu sensei developed thick fingernails and toenails.

which are now sought after by modern researchers of the art. I have never failed to read newfound books, either. Many of these books are about Iga ryu and Koga ryu. Most of the documents or materials being discovered are about these schools.

H: Is that so? Once I read some documents about other ninjutsu schools such as Yasuda ryu or Fukushima ryu, but I don't think those researchers who kept the documents wanted to make them open to the public. I understand why they are unwilling to do so. These documents are mostly about dangerous things like poisonous drugs and so forth.

T: Yes, that's important, too.

H: Regarding the origin of ninjutsu: some say that it already existed in the age of the gods and some insist that it dates from the civil turmoil of the fourteenth through the sixteenth centuries. Which is correct?

T: In the age of gods, it is said that some persons by the names of Amenoshibinomikoto, Kumebe, Otomo, and other ascetics in the Province of Kishu practiced ninjutsu. I hear that my family line comes from a clan in the woods of Takao in Iga Province. Grandfather would often tell me stories.

Takao was located in a mountainous region of Iga and people living there were said to be closely banded together. From this, one might judge that all the members of the clan had training in ninjutsu, but I hear that there were only a small number of the inhabitants who practiced it. According to the theory some Chinese, naturalized in Japan, spread ninjutsu; persons by the name of Cho Busho, Yo Gyokko, and Ikai from the T'ang dynasty have been mentioned.

There is another theory about the origin of ninjutsu. It is said that the Bay of Ise and the Shima Peninsula were infested with pirates, who established their base of operations in the district of Omi (present-day Shiga Prefecture). What is important is that these pirates lived in an age of rival warlords who aspired to conquer the whole country. Fujiwara no Kurodo Saneyuki, one of the leaders of the pirates, was active with the regions of Shima and Kishu as his base of operations and is said to have used kaginawa or hooked rope (one of the ninja tools) as a means of climbing up the walls of a ship or towing a ship. This kaginawa gave rise to kusarigama no jutsu or the techniques of using blade and chain weapons of Kukishin ryu. It also developed into kamayari (a forked spear) to be used for hooking a ship, or hiya (fire arrows) for burning a ship.

H: I see. That can substantiate the theory that ninjutsu originated among pirates, can't it?

T: Yes. This is why some advocate that ninjutsu originated here in Japan and was brought over to China and studied further there.

H: I think it natural that some scholars would advocate the idea of ninjutsu having originated here in Japan.

T: In those days, Iga and Koga were lands of steep mountains and deep valleys largely made up of layers of blue clay called zunenko. These places were unexplored regions and therefore natural strongholds of strategic importance for fugitive warriors, as well as for foreigners, to hide themselves from the enemy. This lasted from the Ashikaga period to the age of chronic civil strife (from mid fourteenth to early sixteenth centuries.

H: They were also secret training spots for the ninja, weren't they?

T: Quite right. There is a rock called Tojin-iwa or Chinese rock over there. I hear that every prayer one offers to this rock is answered. This rock is also called kuji no iwa or rock of kuji. Ninja must have learned and mastered hicho karate koppojutsu from Mother Nature there.

H: You've just said "learned from Mother Nature." These are key words only a ninja could understand.

T: Yes, they are. This idea also improved the ninja's happo hiken or eight methods of secret swords.

Takamatsu sensei said, "My grandmaster, Toda, would often run up a post."

The enemy who is against the laws of nature will lose his battle before he begins to fight. The first priority to the ninja is to win without fighting.

H: Regardless of the times and schools, the ninja seem to have trained in such various things as ninja no hachimon or the eight fields of knowledge; kiai or energy attuning; koppo taijutsu; ninja sword, spear; shuriken or throwing blades; kajutsu or fire technique; yugei or polite accomplishments; kyomon or religious teachings; and ninja juhachi kei or eighteen levels of training.

T: Yes. But since these are peculiar to ninja lore, it is impossible for the public to comprehend them.

H: The ninja are symbolized by the word *shadow*. And some equate ninjutsu with "shadow." Nevertheless, shadow is only a part of tonkei no jutsu or various techniques of hiding including jinton no jutsu (man-hiding), isn't it?

T: It certainly is.

H: During and after the age of the civil war, especially the times of Oda, Toyotomi, and Tokugawa, there was much more dramatic literature on ninjutsu wasn't there?

T: Yes. Momochi Sandayu, Togakure Daisuke, and Ishikawa Goemon were among the most popular characters. Incidentally, Ishikawa Goemon was described as a wrongdoer by people of later years, but as a matter of fact, he wasn't. Records say he kept company with respectable persons. He is said to have been boiled to death in a cauldron, but I don't believe he was caught. Another master ninja named Kidomaru can be mentioned here. Anyway, during the age of civil war, almost all the documents on the part of losers were usually destroyed. Besides, winners might have left records to their advantage, revisions of actual events that make them more benevolent than they really were. This is very important when researching the history of ninja. On the other hand, information handed down by word of mouth can often survive.

H: Generally speaking, approximately when did ninjutsu perfect itself?

T: According to what I heard from my teacher, it perfected itself between the eras of Manju (1024 A.D.) and Shoho (1074 A.D.).

H: I see. People are often prejudiced against the ninja. I think this is because only those who are unfamiliar with what ninjutsu really is dare dramatize or depict the ninja in novels.

T: I quite agree with you. There were very few ninjas in the true sense of the word. In the age of civil wars many died before they could become master ninjas.

H: Is that so? Over a decade has passed since I started to learn under your guidance, but my ninjutsu is still far from perfect.

T: In the age of gods, Emperor Jinmu placed Okume no mikoto in charge of shinobu ho or the art of stealth. Okume no mikoto left one of his retainers in Kishu to make him take an active role in the services of shinobu ho. I hear this retainer initiated warrior-ascetics visiting Kumano in Kishu into the art of stealth. Everyone knows the story of Yamato Takeru no Mikoto who, by utilizing shinobu ho, put down a rebellion of Kumaso, disguising himself as a woman. Shotoku Taishi, or the Crown Prince Shotoku (574–622 A.D.), is said to have used shinobi or ninja, too, when establishing the state.

There are other records left referring to the ninja. The monk Dokyo (?–772) was condemned to exile by Okuma Wake no Kiyomaro, a very loyal servant of the Crown, who stood in his way. Dokyo dispatched fifteen assassins to kill Kiyomaro on his way to Okuma. However, Kiyomaro's bodyguards—Otomo brothers called Komaro and Take-maro—who were masters of ninjutsu, kenpo, and bojutsu, killed all the assassins. The bujutsu employed then was recorded in the scroll of Ryusen no maki about which I have already told you. This scroll contains descriptions of ninjutsu, shuriken, and kusarigama.

H: Yes, I know about it. Ninjutsu took root in the Iga or Koga Provinces and has been handed down in various forms. For instance, the densho scroll of Kumogakure ryu ninpo describes Sarutobi Sasuke who was an expert at jumping from branch to branch like a monkey by using a forked spear.

T: Precisely. In olden times as a person was represented by the name of the area where he lived, so was he called after the jutsu he mastered. We cannot miss this point when we study the history of ninjutsu.

H: In an age when the existence of one's genealogy is life-threatening, one would naturally destroy it. On the contrary, when one's genealogy is much thought of, he may resort to artifices to make it apparently better. In the case of ninja genealogies, we often find space with no names written there. This means that they had left them unrecorded until suitable successors appeared, doesn't it?

T: Yes, it does. If we judge based on records only, we may commit a grave blunder.

Well, let me go back to the subject of ninjutsu. As shinobu ho or

Iga Ueno province.

shinobu waza (the art of stealth) came to be called ninjutsu, true ninjas began to realize that they should be enlightened on the laws of humanity. They tried to avoid unreasonable conflicts or fighting. I learned from my master that the ninjas' duty is to be enlightened on the laws of humanity. There should be no fighting that does not follow these rules. Therefore, the enemy who stands against the laws of nature has lost his battle before he begins the fight. The first priority to the ninja was to win without fighting, and that remains the way.

I have learned this by heart. People can't wake up to the realization of this before they experience any kind of trials. You must keep this in mind, Hatsumi-san. It will gradually come home to your heart and then turn into perspiration. The perspiration will evaporate going up into heaven and the god Kami will teach you many things through the vapor.

Today eighteen years since Takamatsu sensei passed away, I often talk with him in heaven while giving lessons to my students, wet with perspiration. The conversation between us goes on secretly and soundlessly. I continue this with all my heart and mind:

Sensei! Now I understand why you called me Hatsumi sensei. A certain artist says, "Man spends his first forty years in learning and training, the next thirty years in meeting a trial, and thereafter in seeing his best days." I was fortunate enough to be able to meet you when you were seventy years old. This means I could have training surrounded by your beautiful flowers. I felt as if I trained in a flower garden instead of a training hall. When I made a mistake in training, you said to me, "I am to blame for it, because I didn't teach you that."

I now understand what you meant. You intended to tell me that I should have a sense of gezashin (a guilty conscience) and gratitude. I must offer you both gezashin and gratitude. From now on I will see my students with these two senses. You were my only teacher, which made me feel even sadder when you passed away. I know very well how deep the sorrow of one's separation from his teacher is. It is equal to that of one's parting from his parents. For this reason, I told one of my disciples not to become a teacher. But to my great regret, he left me without trying to know my true intention. Nevertheless, it is my hearty wish that my disciples become good teachers.

People say kenzen-ichijo, namely, the sword and zen should go hand in hand. But when zen was corrupted, there arose a cry for revival through a love of the poetic. What has become of this kenzen-ichijo today? I, for one, know the situation well, but I think it better to leave it unsaid here. I would rather change the meaning of kenzen-ichijo into

The densho of the Fukushima ryu ninjutsu, left; Ninpiden, or the secret documents of ninjutsu, right.

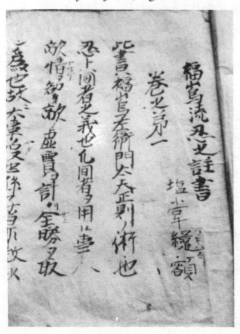
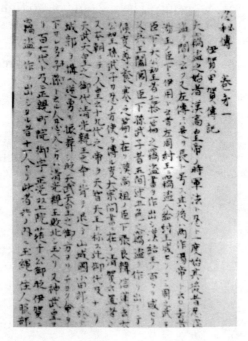

"the sword and the good should go hand in hand." (In this case, *zen* means the good, but both are phonetically the same.) What was also thought highly of was bunbu ryodo, namely, unification of literary and military arts. But it should be changed into another bunbu ryodo, meaning moral and military arts, in view of today's frequent violence.

In my opinion, sword and art should go together, despite Plato's idea of art being banished from the state in order to found an ideal country. The martial arts of Japan have been spreading in the world and "weathering" in each place where they have taken root. This is attributable to the wind of the times. True martial artists should take this as a natural phenomenon. It appears that very few can appreciate this reality. Some say that what will be needed for a leader of martial artists is hakuryoku or power. If I am allowed to put it in my own way, this could be another hakuryoku, meaning a wide range of power. Without such flexibility, one cannot be a leader in the true sense of the word.

Speaking of hakuryoku, there exists a power of never being indignant, doesn't there? Recently, I am surprised to be able to keep my presence of mind even when I get very angry. I think this is because I have acquired what Takamatsu sensei called one of the cool courages. Such being the case, I sometimes try to drive some of my disciples into a passion on purpose in order to give them a chance to see what cool courage is. But there are some who leave me without realizing it.

These days an increasing number of seekers of ninjutsu are coming to the Bujinkan training hall. I would like to give them a line from the *Divine Comedy* by Dante: "Abandon all hope, ye who enter here."

What's this all about? It is a warning to those who are too egotistic and too narrow-minded to attain spiritual enlightenment. But I consider them to be a godsend and hope for them to be able to experience spiritual awakening. I told my disciples to be noble minded. For, since early times, noblemen are supposed to have been wise, beautiful, cultured, economically strong, and influential. Then what about adding "virtue" to the sword and the art? This is a trinity of the sword, art, and virtue.

Let me drop a hint of thinking to those who are fond of fighting—wars, for example. The tragedy of war lies in the fact that not only does it bring us death and destruction, but it produces merchants of death who try to make a profit from it. This rule holds true of the world of martial arts. The more people want to fight, the more people make a profit from it. Never allow yourselves to dance to the music of such fellows. Am I not right, Takamatsu sensei?

"Yes, you are right. All the movies and books have to do is to make profits, isn't it?" he replied, smiling again. You will be laughed at by owls unless you know such a thing. When you walk through the dark world of desires, owls can be your good guides. A true ninja can see through everything in the world of desires.

Today there are as many disciples of mine throughout the world as there are stars in the night sky. Indeed, they became pupils of mine in search of a smiling sun and I am sure I taught them how to get it. But I wonder if there are some who have disappeared just like stardust or shooting stars outside the constellation.

Let me show you part of the teachings of Saint Nichiren (1222-82), the founder of the Hokke (Lotus) sect of Buddhism:

> My fellowmen! Even in distress, if you follow the teachings without harboring a doubt, you will be able to attain spiritual enlightenment and will not have to regret your worldly unhappiness. But however hard I may preach—day in, day out—those who harbor a doubt will be lost in a maze and cannot notice they are heading for hell.

I am sure the ninja's night journey leads to daybreak. I remember the day vividly in my mind when I stayed at Takamatsu sensei's house and saw him the next morning clapping his hands in worship toward the rising sun.

I am now over fifty years old, nearly sixty. It was only recently that I suddenly realized what I was, when considering ninpo and martial arts. Let me quote from Miyamoto Musashi's *Book of Five Rings*: "Since

A hundred poems by ninja Yoshimori.

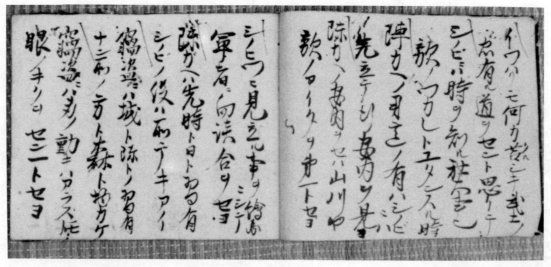

then, I trained myself every day in the morning and in the evening in order to find profound truth. I finally mastered the art of combat at the age of fifty or so." In this regard, Musashi and I have had similar experiences. I also believe life begins at fifty.

A long time ago, Oda Nobunaga, a military ruler, said that a man's life lasted fifty years. Those who do not know how warriors think, believe that man's span of life is over at fifty. But this is incorrect. What he meant was that a warrior was able to fight with physical strength until the age of fifty. Then, his real life would begin. I think it is better to succeed in business after the age of fifty. In gaining success at an early age, there is every probability that you will ultimately fail, because of the desire for yondoku—women, liquor, money, and power.

Through the teachings of Takamatsu sensei's martial arts, I found a life. And now I realize that the life has settled in my mind. A righteous life is more precious than a thousand-carat diamond. Once Takamatsu sensei said to me, "Ninja should have the benevolence to protect men of justice since there are lots of good and respectable people in the world." Now I have been enjoying two lives, one provided by Mother Nature and the other by Takamatsu sensei. Assuming man's life ends at fifty years, my life is already over. Then the rest of my life is the one provided by Takamatsu sensei. Thus, as a fortunate man who can take good care of his righteous life, I will live the rest of my life in all sincerity. To fulfill this purpose, I will paint and enjoy music. Some worldlings may ask me, "What's the good of your doing such things?" I reply, "What I mean is just like the sennin or the hermit who lives on air. As the sennin lives on wonderful pictures of Mother Nature and makes the singing of birds and the sight of animals his mental food, so do the ninja."

A certain German poet said, "No worldling is so narrow-minded as a specialist." Today people are being captivated by the natural food boom. Let me tell you that true natural food should be natural beauty or ninja air.

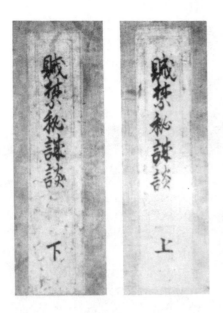

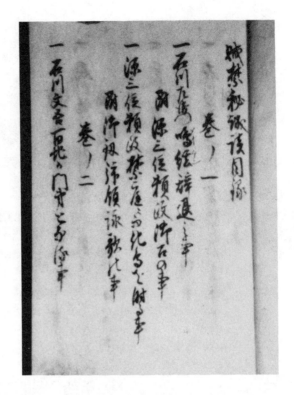

The documents in which Ishikawa Goemon and Momochi Sandayu are mentioned. These copies were seemingly written in the Edo era.

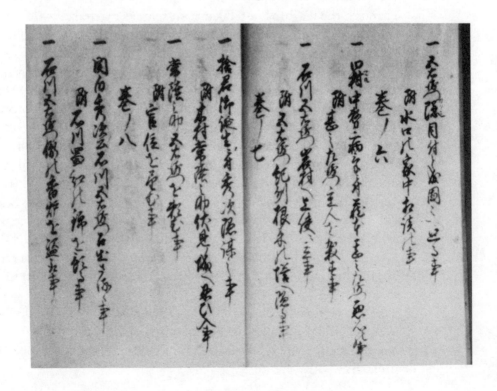

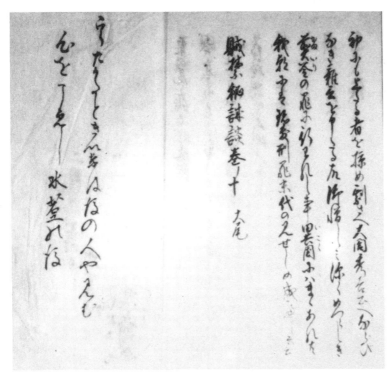

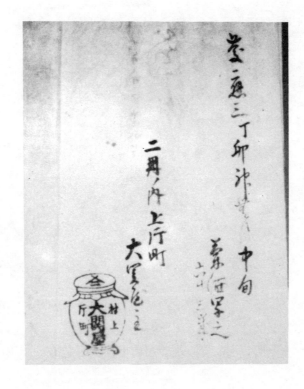

一　附章武部石川の不儀を志す事

一　石川謀て義輝公を殺す事
　附百姓の世倩武部を殺す由申入る事

巻ノ三

一　百姓の世倩汚名を次ぐ謀書事
　附百姓三走文并肖を倩む事
一　石川父吾百姓の世倩を殺し立退事
　附伊賀郡城比事

巻ノ四

一　本行章陸奥童を石川の智子と成す事
　附荒野但馬守伏見へ行く事
一　石川太郎氏鑑、盗織小遣入る事
　附役人を斬り捕る事

巻ノ五

一　石川公お後、世芸寺中網公廠を剝す事
　附石川椿座へ悪ひ入る事

巻二應三丁卯沖　中旬

二期ノ内上斤町
大寶庵

Kotora and Kanzaki

Takamatsu sensei was called Kotora (little tiger) when he was about fifteen years old, attending an English school in Kobe. On his way back home one day, he stopped at the exercise hall of Shinryuken Toda sensei. Toda sensei said to Kotora, "You arrived just in time. Hitotsubashi and Kanzaki, both taijutsu masters of the Musashi School, have just challenged us to a match. Kotora, will you go against them?"

"Yes, I will," said Kotora.

Kotora first went against Hitotsusbashi, overpowering him with spiritual strength. It seemed he was using a form of Shirabegata or observing the opponent's move. Kotora built up spiritual pressure against him slowly but steadily. Hitotsubashi was overwhelmed and tried to strike at a vital part of Kotora's chest with his right fist. Kotora warded off the blow with his right hand and took a low posture—the form sensei—to kick him down.

Hitotsubashi jumped.

At the very moment Hitotsubashi was ready to catch Kotora from the air in a counterattack with hands and feet, Kotora uttered a spirited kiai. Hitotsubashi fell headlong, with such an impact that it

31

sounded as if the floor was broken. Hitotsubashi fainted.

Watching the scene, Kanzaki stood up. As in the previous match, Kotora and his opponent stared at each other face to face, applying spiritual pressure. Kanzaki was a 29-year-old genius, who was called the kishin of the Musashi school. He was even permitted to confer full mastership in taijutsu of the Kanzaki Musashi school. Both thought, "He is my equal." And for a while they competed with their eyes and mental power.

Suddenly, Kanzaki's right hand leaped out, but this was a feint. Kotora, who was young and confident, reacted, expecting a blow from Kanzaki's right hand, swinging his left hand, but was trapped. Kanzaki struck fiercely at the left elbow joint with the side of his hand.

Disregarding the broken elbow, Kotora instantly counterattacked with a technique called gyaku ganseki otoshi (throwing the opponent to the ground head first). Kanzaki could not stand and collapsed.

Kotora thought, "I did it." But in that moment, he felt dizzy and fell to the floor.

In the taijutsu of the Musashi school, one allows his opponent to feel he has won. The opponent thinks, "I made it," and at that moment drops his guard, one then takes advantage of this unguarded moment and gains the final victory.

However, Kanzaki could not avoid the crushing gyaku ganseki otoshi applied by Kotora, and was knocked out.

On the other hand, Kotora was also suffering from an attack to the ears and left arm. The joint of the arm was dislocated and he too passed out. Toda sensei brought both fighters back to consciousness. After they came around they shared the pleasure of having had a good fight. Kanzaki said, "I have had seven or eight matches on my way from Tokyo to Kyoto on the Tokaido and I've never been defeated. I am amazed at my loss as Toda sensei told me that you were only fifteen years old." Then, Kotora and Kanzaki enthusiastically discussed characteristics of taijutsu of the Musashi school.

Young masters who pursue the same martial arts can talk endlessly.

3
Genjutsu and Yojutsu: Illusions, Tricks, and the Supernatural

There are similar tricks in genjutsu, ninjutsu, and yojutsu but there are differences. In order to give the correct image of the ninja and ninjutsu and to differentiate between the three jutsu, let me introduce you to genjutsu and yojutsu. People who perform genjutsu are called magicians, illusionists (genjutsushi), and rainmakers. They are influenced by Mikkyo (secret teachings of Dainichi Nyorai) and dokyo or Taoism. (The character for "yo" in yojutsu can be defined as doubtful, strange, or supernatural.) In comparison with genjutsu, yojutsu is eerie and performs its tricks by borrowing the supernatural powers of the various spirits. Of course, the ninja also perform tricks that may be classified as the aforementioned categories of jutsu.

In the Kyojitsu Zatsudanshu written in the second year of Kansei (1790), it is recorded that a genjutsu master by the name of Kashinkyoshi was active between the Muromachi (1500) and Azuchi Momoyama period. Kashinkyoshi performed such tricks or miracles as making the wife of a samurai who had been dead for five years, appear in front of the widower's eyes. Another illusion was performed at a drinking party in the town of Nara. The townsmen at the party asked the master to show them an illusion, so the master flooded the hall with water and

Acting as thieves aiming at conquering a country, these characters appeared in popular literature.

made a water dragon appear. The townsmen for fear of drowning and being attacked by the dragon all fainted. But when they regained consciousness the hall had no evidence of the flood or of the dragon.

Once he scared lord Oda Nobunaga by showing him a man in hell being gruesomely tortured. In the presence of another heroic warrior, Toyotomi Hideyoshi, he showed an illusion that hurt the pride of the short-tempered lord. For this, the master was to be crucified. When he was pinned to the cross, the executioner asked him what his last wish was. The master replied that although he had performed many tricks and transformed himself into various animals, he had never transformed himself into the form of a mouse; so as his last wish in this existence he wanted to perform the illusion of becoming a mouse. Then, he asked the executioner to loosen the rope for him. He transformed himself into a mouse and climbed to the top of the crucifixion post. Without a moment's notice, a hawk dove from high in the sky and grasped the mouse in his sharp claws.

The great master illusionist became a meal for a hawk. It can be said that his search for the ultimate illusion just for his own satisfaction made him lose perspective on his life and finally led to his death.

A genjutsu master named Kato Danzo, also called flying Kato, was performing the trick of swallowing a cow in front of a large crowd of people. When a man in the crowd saw through his trick, Kato compensated for this by sowing some moonflower seeds on the ground. Right after hitting the ground they began to sprout, the vines grew out, buds formed and then bloomed. The moonflower blossoms are said to have been seventy centimeters wide. While the crowd was astonished by the moonflower blossoms, the head of the man who had seen through the trick fell to the ground with a loud noise, then his body fell, split in two.

Hearing of the illusionist's reputation, the warrior lord, Uesugi Kenshin called on him to come to the castle. The lord asked him if he was the master illusionist. Kato replied that he was indeed the master illusionist and with his powers nothing was impossible. So the lord challenged him to sneak into the mansion of Naoeyamashiro no kami, one of the lord's vassals, and steal his long sword. The illusionist immediately headed for the mansion. Before he left, Kenshin ordered his vassals to guard the mansion, placing guards at various posts, placing lights to eliminate the advantage of darkness, and letting loose a band of furious guard dogs. The guards stayed alert throughout the night. But the illusionist used don kenjutsu and donjinjutsu (the trick of swallowing entire dogs and humans) and appeared in the presence of the lord as promised with the long sword.

The lord was impressed by the master illusionist and thought that he would be a tremendous asset against an enemy if he were to be the lord's vassal. But also he was a great danger if he were to turn against him and disobey orders. Useful as a beast is useful when in chains, but when the chain breaks he would be as dangerous as a freed beast. Seeing this side of the situation the lord said that the illusionist was a threat to the populace and ordered his execution. Quickly sensing the turn of events, Kato attempted to flee. But in a moment, he was surrounded by enemies on all sides.

Pretending to have given up his attempt, he said "Now, everyone, I would like to show you something amazing." He pulled out a gourd and appeared as though he was pouring sake wine into the cup. About twenty little dolls came out of the gourd and started to dance. The amusing little dance of the dolls captivated the vassals. In a few moments, the dolls had disappeared and so had the illusionist.

After this episode, the master illusionist visited Takeda Shingen, another powerful lord. Again, the lord declared the illusionist a threat

Right, the Laws of Genjutsu; left, Ninjutsu and Yojutsu.

and ordered his vassals to execute him. It is told that he was either decapitated or shot.

Some say that because an illusionist uses devious tricks, he must have a wicked heart. We must realize that these tricks, used to deceive people, were taught for that purpose; thus the performers gain a wicked heart by training in them. There are many theories about the behavior of these illusionists but as a ninja they are of no interest to me. It is enough for me to understand the basic nature of genjutsu. Through words the illusionist leads the audience into a hallucinatory state. As if in a dream or by a trick of the imagination, a deceased wife appears; by hypnosis townsmen are swept over by a great flood.

Let me explain why Flying Kato failed to deceive a member of the audience when he performed the cow-swallowing trick. He failed because his spirit was not strong enough to absorb the full attention of the audience. Also there are people who are hypnotized easily and those who are hard to hypnotize. To explain his other trick, let me say that there are some types of moonflowers that act as hallucinogens. In the ancient views on illusionary tricks, it is understood that the illusions are performed by the will of the performer overpowering the spirit and body of the audience—controlling and surpressing its ability to resist his suggestions. By controlling their actions and thoughts, the illusionist makes them move at his will and inserts the image of his vision into

Supernatural power is not a skill or a trick. It exists
in your heart, in your sincerity.

their minds. Striking terror into the audiences' hearts or filling them
with illusionary joy is a type of mass hypnosis.

Yojutsu, supernatural tricks, can be classified into various categories:
giraiya, using toads; daijamaru, riding on giant snakes; tsunadehime,
riding on slugs; and otomowakanahime, using spiders. All of these
animals live in dark places and are generally disliked.

Yojutsu plays an active role in the world of kabuki theatre. Supernatural tricks in the theatre may have been a means of defiance toward the
ones in power. The curtain on the Japanese stage is opened sideways by
an opener in the wings instead of the curtains being pulled up. These
curtains are unique in the world. If one calls genjutsu spacial illusion
tricks, yojutsu should be called material tricks. But let me declare that
they only exist in the realm of fantasy. When you finish training in the
ways of the ninja, your piercing eyes can see through the trivial tricks of
yojutsu and genjutsu as natural phenomenona applied for the purpose
of illusion. One night, Takamatsu sensei told me this tale of the time he
was training at a temple on Mount Hiei.

Takamatsu sensei happened to hear from a group of priests at the
temple that "In Shishinden, terrifying monsters appear at night, so no
one dares to go there."

Replying to this he said, "What are you saying! I'll go there and see
what the 'monster' really is." He took the night watch alone and spent a
night at Shishinden. When the lights had been turned off and a warm
breeze swept through, as if calling the monsters to appear, he started to
nod off. But then, he heard a drum sound its sorrowful tone. "So, the
monster has appeared," he said and quietly listened for where the sound
came from. It seemed to come from under the building. Using the
wind-like moving method of the ninja, he sneaked into the space
between the floor and the earth, about one meter in height. With the
light from outside, he used ankokutoshi no jutsu (a method that
enables one to see in darkness) and saw a shadow.

Unbelievable as it was, there was a large frog, almost thirty centimeters wide, using the drum to attract insects. At this moment he remembered a story he heard from his teacher, Toda sensei. In olden times,
ninjas used to let frogs free under the floors of the enemy lord to

The eye of a camera sometimes creates illusionary images just as genjutsu or yojutsu does.

psychologically weaken him by attacking his nerves with the noise. So the much-feared monster was only a large frog.

Takamatsu sensei has told me many stories from his time at Mount Hiei. Once he was having a discussion with a friend, a Buddhist priest, when a lizard, in his wobbling gait, ran along the railing in the hall. He willed the lizard to fall off the railing and land on its back by giving a single yell. The lizard was unconscious for a while but swiftly disappeared when it awoke. They resumed their discussion after this. Half an hour later, the lizard returned and was now wobbling along the floor. He gave another yell and the lizard turned over on its stomach in surprise. This time he did not let go of the lizard and paralyzed it with fudo kanashibari no jutsu (a method that paralyzes the victim with a spell). The priest was amazed at seeing such a trick twice in a row. At that time, he was enlightened to the astonishing power of the will.

Sometime later, Takamatsu sensei saw a wagtail flying from branch to branch in the temple yard. He gave a single yell and the bird dropped to the ground flopping about unable to fly away. An elder priest who saw this was thoroughly impressed with Takamatsu's willpower. He asked him to become the head priest for Chusenji temple.

A master ninja can see through the tricks of yojutsu or genjutsu. Even a great master of these tricks will not be able to surprise the ever-calm ninja. Let me mention here that the ninjas utilize yojutsu and genjutsu in inton jutsu (hiding techniques) and in intrigue.

Here, I have illustrated the relationship between ninjutsu and genjutsu. In order to realize the fundamental characteristics of ninjutsu please observe the illustration carefully.

Ninjutsu Daihi Seishintoitsu Shuyouikkan

Sacred Methods of Ninjutsu to Gain An Overpowering Will

NINJUTSU

- Shinto Hiho (Secret teachings of Shinto)
- Hachimon tonko jujutsu (Eight methods of incantation)
- Taijutsusosoku Shugyo (Body technique of walking like the wind)
  - Mutodorijutsu (Capturing without using a sword)
  - Senbannage and Kodachi (Techniques for disk harpoons and small swords)
  - Jissensekko Gijutsu (Techniques of scouting in actual battle)

GENJUTSU

- Buddhism, especially Mikkyo (Secret teachings of Dainichi Nyorai)
- Senjutsudokyo (Teachings of mountain sages)
- Taijutsu Sosokushugyo (The body technique of walking like the wind)
  - Shuriken and Kodachi (Throwing blade and small sword)
  - Heigaku no ichibu (A portion of war strategies)
  - Shugendo and Sekkojutsu (Mountaineering asceticism and scouting techniques)

Genjutsu arrived in Japan in the Nara period from India through China and Korea. It is also said that it was a performing art in the Muromachi period.

Genjutsu arrived in Japan in the Nara period from India through China and Korea. It is also said that it was a performing art in the Muromachi period.

After seeing my body techniques and martial arts methods, some people call me a magician. I have written many books but I do not think I can express the true nature of my teachings on paper. For instance, I explain a technique by photographs and add descriptions that go along with them, but I feel that this is not nearly enough. The movements that should come in the white space between the photographs are important. The surrounding white space can be said to be a veil in white smoke, the wisdom and spirit of the master ninja.

When I see performers of genjutsu or yojutsu, perhaps using the mental power of a snake or some other trick, I want to tell them to hibernate until the world becomes springlike. The ninja would like to tell them to awaken to the spring world of light and to abandon their dark world. Give up rancor and hatred. A warm spring wind breezes through the heart of all who forget their grudges and in those hearts love grows. In the presence of love, magic tricks do not fool.

The Sumo Wrestlers

Kotaro at age 13 was striving every day in his practice of the art of Kotoryu koppojutsu and for a license from the Shindenfudo ryo. At the time, he weighed 132 pounds. In those days lawn sumo was popular: from the time they were 14 or 15, and up to about the age of 20, young men in all the provinces held sumo tournaments nightly. One night at Inariyama, a sumo tournament was announced. Kotaro went there to watch. There were many people gathered, their wild enthusiasm and cheers echoed off the mountain. Making his way through the crowd, Kotaro sat at the front edge of the earthen arena. A large man, nicknamed Oni no yama (Demon Mountain), who had defeated several wrestlers, was about to fight with Raiden (Thunder Lightning).

"In the east, Raiden; in the west, Oni no yama," the referee called out. The wrestlers grappled with one another and just after the referee pulled the judging plaque, Demon Mountain pulled Thunder Lightning down with a jerk. Thunder Lightning simply fell down. Following this, Demon Mountain grasped Thunder Lightning's belt, turned sideways and threw him out of the arena.

The sumo bug within Kotaro began to rave. He was too impatient

41

to even take off his clothes and put on a belt. Fully clothed, he climbed into the ring, answering the shout of Oni no yama, calling for a challenger.

The referee asked for his name.

He replied, "I am Akebono."

The referee announced, "In the east, Onino yama; in the west, Akebono." Onino yama came at him with full force. Moving from the focus of Oni no yama's aim, Jutaro threw him. One after another, taking only a wink of an eye's time, Akebono beat eight men of 22 or 23 years of age. There seemed to be no one who could surpass him.

Suddenly, there appeared a huge man weighing 248 pounds. He announced himself as Osakayama and climbed into the ring. This was a battle between a 248-pound man and a 132-pound teenager. As is often the case, in a battle between a small wrestler and a huge one the audience rooted for the small one. The yells for Akebono were loud enough to make the mountains shake.

"In the east, Osakayama; In the west, Akebono." The cheers heightened in the excitement. The two glared at one another and the referee signaled with the plaque for them to begin. They collided with a crunch and stood trying to grab each other's belt. No matter how hard Akebono tried to push or pull with his full force. Osakayama would not budge. Osakayama grabbed his right hand and pushed forcefully. Akebono, using Osakayama's thrust, tried to catch him with a wrist throw. Attempting to regain his balance, Osakayama blundered and stepped out of the ring with his right foot. The referee raised the plaque high in the air and announced the winner, "Akebono!" Seeing this the crowd cheered madly and threw their sitting mats and haori-coats high in the air.

The next day Osakayama came to see Kotaro's father Yasaburo. "I am actually Kokumonryu (Black-gate Dragon), a sumo wrestler from Osaka. Please let me raise your son to become a sumo wrestler," said the man.

Yasaburo answered, "Thank you for coming from so far away. I must decline your offer because I am raising my son to become a soldier." Only at this admission by the huge man did they know that Kotaro, at thirteen years of age, had beaten a professional sumo wrestler.

4
Ninpo Through Camera Eyes

I have tried to produce motion pictures of ninpo movements or those of other martial arts using high-speed photographic technology and to prove the facts on behalf of the ninpo and other martial arts researchers and trainees. A camera is disadvantaged in comparison to a human being, as the former has only one eye while the latter two! Despite the imbalance or inaccuracy a camera may have, I dared to display ninpo through camera eyes. On the other hand, in sumo games, a slow-motion video sometimes makes a correct judgment and proves the judge to have been wrong. This indicates that the eye of a camera is sometimes more reliable than that of a man.

One day, a karate master told a cameraman that when he broke a pile of roof tiles with his hand, the middle or the bottom tiles would break first, but not the top one. Then, twenty roof tiles were actually piled up with a towel on the top of them (for the purpose of protecting his hands). The karate master started breathing in, breathing out, and dealt a blow to the piled tiles. Against the master's expectation, the video showed that the tiles had broken from the top to the bottom in order.

Another example is an archery master I met. He believed that when he drew a bow like a full moon and released it, the arrow would go

43

A photograph worth $10,000 taken by Mr. Hashi.

first, hardly before the string was released. However, when the film was actually taken and his movements were reproduced in slow motion, he found that the arrow had been shaped like a crescent moon by the force of the bowstring before it had flown away. The camera convinced both the karate master and the archery master of their errors.

These incidents show how often trainees in martial arts can be overconfident or blindly possessed by whatever they call "belief"—right or wrong. They can get brainwashed during training and unconsciously take a step in the wrong direction.

I am often asked for manuscripts or photographs of ninjutsu and martial arts by several U.S. magazines. I do my best to meet their wishes, but one day, the chief editor of *Ninja* magazine complained to me, "We don't want any pictures without faces shown on them."

I responded, "Your U.S. martial arts magazines are making a big mistake handling these pictures as you do. You do not seem to understand what the most important thing is in martial arts. What I always try to do is focus on the important points." The pictures in these magazines seem only to emphasize dreadful faces, muscular bodies, or such, as if the appearance showed what the person could actually do. Pictures of killers seem to have the most appeal to U.S. readers. These magazines are not portraying an art, but an "attraction"—the artist rather than his art.

I try to let people see in my pictures what the martial art really is—not depending on appearance—and to change the wrong conceptions about martial arts American people generally have. Fortunately, what I said was fully understood and appreciated by him.

One day Mr. Kondo Sosaku, a famous film director for a very popular TV series "Judo Story" visited me, offering to introduce ninpo to the world on video. I accepted his offer.

They used three video cameras to film all my movements, saying that one would not be enough. Three eyes were watching me from three angles. Once they asked, "Would you please repeat that movement again?"

I replied that I could never perform a movement more than once. If I did the same thing twice, the movement would become just a "pattern." Even if it looks like the same movement, only the slightest difference either in my action or in that of my opponent may change the situation completely. For example, from the starting point you draw a right angle. If this right angle is 0.001 degree incorrect, the line will be more and more inaccurate as it goes farther from the starting point. The same process occurs in a ninpo demonstration.

The three films were edited into one. Seeing the film, the director said to me, "You defeat the opponent so easily that it doesn't look very appealing."

Although he was much impressed and seemed deeply moved by the complete film, he still looked unsatisfied after my narration was recorded, saying that there were too many things that puzzled him.

Television cameras have a difficult time recording taijutsu motions.

And he added that he would use five cameras next time, as three did not seem to work. He would set one camera under a glass floor and the other above me.

The movements of ninpo are essentially not appealing to one's vision. There always exist lots of movements that could not possibly be reproduced on video. It is not a matter of distance. No matter how close you are to your teacher when learning from him, no matter how many details he shows you, a great part of ninpo cannot be explained. Ninpo is indeed a deep art.

The director, Kondo, laughed and told me "Your movements cannot be caught by our old legendary single-eyed goblin or even by our high-technology three-eyed goblin. They are no match for you at all."

I have had quite a few chances to meet a good many professional photographers, through which I often make unexpected discoveries. For example, when I coached the actors at a rehearsal for the play titled *The Ninja*, the director, the writer, and the producer of the play happened to be together. A newspaper reporter and a cameraman rushed to them for an interview. The reporter asked the cameraman to take several pictures from various angles. The cameraman asked how many pictures would appear on the newspaper, and he answered that he would use only one for the evening paper. Their conversation had hardly finished when the cameraman clicked the shutter just once and strode away from the scene, leaving the astonished reporter behind.

Even now I remember clearly how much I was impressed by his self-confidence as a professional.

Early in the history of Japan, there was a famous power struggle between two big families, the Genji and the Heike. This happened during the battle of Itsukushima led by the young Genji leader, Yoshitsune.

A boat was floating on the ocean. A folding fan was tied on the pole fixed at the end of the boat. The Heike's samurai found a woman on the boat standing under the fan, and teased the Genji samurai, daring them to shoot down the fan. Yoshitsune heard the Heike's samurai insult his men and asked them, "Can someone shoot it down?"

Nasu Yoichi, the best archer among Genji's young samurais, brought his horse forward and drew a bow. The boat was rolling. The fan was dancing. His failure would be a disgrace to the whole family for many years to come. Just as the ninja do before using ninjutsu, he meditated and chanted to himself. He let loose an arrow that struck the target dead center and brought the fan down. Like the cameraman, only one shot was necessary.

There is always something in common between any two arts.

I have talked to a professional camerawoman who specializes in taking pictures of horses. What she said about them was very much like a ninjutsu fifth godan test.

Let me tell you briefly how the godan test is done: A judge holds up a sword. An examinee sits in front of him with his back to the judge. The judge utters a few words to mark the start and cuts unexpectedly at the trainee's head. The trainee must dodge it in a fraction of a second.

According to this photographer, if you aim your camera at him, a horse is so conscious of being watched that he will never give you a chance for a good shot. So she turns her back on him instead. When the horse relaxes and moves freely as he wants to, she suddenly turns around to take the pictures. She said to me that it was how she could take wonderful pictures of horses.

The mysterious parts of ninpo suggest its profundity. However, a photographer with great technique and skills would be able to express in a picture the essence of ninpo.

When I travelled in New York, I met a famous photographer, Mr. Hashi. It costs ten thousand dollars to have just one shot taken by him. So I told him at the seminar that one movement I would make would cost ten thousand dollars, too. The trainees there said in chorus, "He is right!" And I had him take four pictures.

A spirit seen around my ear—at the Foreign Press Club.

Sometimes one can see in a picture the spirit of Zen, Ichigo Ichie. *Ichigo* means a whole life and *Ichie* one chance. You meet someone whom you may never see again. It may be the only chance to meet him in your life. That is exactly why you should receive him sincerely and do all you can do for him at that moment. A great photograph expresses Ichigo Ichie.

One day I received a letter in which a picture of me demonstrating ninpo at a press club was enclosed. The letter said:

> Dear Master Hatsumi,
>   I happened to find your address in the newspaper yesterday and decided to write to you. I was deeply impressed by the TV program in which you and Mr. Masaaki Ishikawa appeared last year. Later, I had a chance to see you perform Ninjutsu at the foreign reporters club and took the enclosed picture. Unfortunately it was not very clear in the darkness. But you can see your guiding spirit around your ear in this picture. This spirit is Mr. Chosokabe, a samurai of the Toyotomi family, with a neatly-shaven beard, in his fifties. Some people may say

that it is just a blurred photograph. But his face is so clear. I do believe that some have a supernatural power.

I am looking forward to another opportunity to see you, when I would love to take a clearer spiritual picture. People who engage in martial arts can concentrate more easily than others, so it seems to be possible to take spiritual pictures if a photographer can concentrate at the same time.

I lost no time in visiting the sender of the letter accompanied by one of my trainees Fumio Manaka. I said, "Thank you so much for your letter and picture. How did you take the picture?"

"You took a breath when you threw a hand sword. At this moment, I took a breath, too, and pressed the shutter."

"How do you know that my guiding spirit is a samurai named Chosokabe?"

"I looked at the picture very closely. My spiritual telepathy made me see the letters 'Chosokabe' on the picture."

"That's something! As you said, the book my late teacher gave me refers to his name!"

"Yes, I believe you are somehow related to him."

"Does one have only one spirit close by?"

"No. If you do another bujutsu, a different spirit may be around you."

"Take his picture, too, then."

After I left him, I went to one of my friends, Suya, who is a novelist and doctor, and told him about my remarkable conversation.

I asked him, "What do you think of spirits? Some people say that a spirit named Isobe was wandering behind Yukio Mishima," a famous writer who killed himself.

"Someone like me who has been long engaged in natural science cannot believe in spirits. But I can accept the concept of reincarnation," he said.

"I dare say that I am half negative and half affirmative," I responded.

The other day, I also called Professor Masaaki Ishikawa about spiritual photographs. He said, "If you do some trick on the film in the developing process, you can easily make a blurred picture that looks like a spirit."

When he saw the picture, he also said, "I am sure that this is just a trick of light. You remember that there were three spotlights beaming toward you, don't you?"

All living creatures as well as human beings lose instinct and awareness of their subconscious as the level of culture becomes higher and higher. And finally, we lose this intuition that is so essential for living. Very few people actually know about the nature of spirit. Some religious organizations sometimes take advantage of this blind spot and force or threaten the followers. These organizations are not worthy of being called religions at all.

My late master Takamatsu used to say, "Supernatural power is not a skill or trick. It exists in your heart, in your sincerity. Religion is the same, too."

We human beings may be great devils that threaten or confuse others by using skills or tricks. But religion is not for deceiving or threatening people. Religion is equal to one's sincerity. I will continue my study on spirits from the heart, from this sincerity.

I personally want to believe in spirits. There are millions of people in this world who do not seem to have souls or spirits at all. I strongly hope that they will recover their own spirits and lead a more fruitful life.

Let me relate one last, brief experience, having to do with the eye of the camera, I've had recently. This provided me a chance to realize what a secret kiai (energy-attuning yell) is like. When we are practicing, nobody is allowed to take photographs in the training hall, because the flare of the flash is likely to blind us. However, we often have visitors who ignore our warnings. Taking advantage of an interpreter's absence, they take photographs deliberately. I do not dare to stop them if they do so for their own study. But some are using their photographs for business. These people do not pay attention to our difficulties.

One day a professional cameraman visited our training hall and thoughtlessly began to take photographs. Then, I dared to send him a secret kiai for the purpose of interrupting the flash. Three days later, I met with the cameraman in front of my house. Uttering the words, "No pictures came out well," he showed his photographs to me. Half of them were black and the other half out of focus. "I'm a first-rate professional, so why all this?"

"That's because I had sent you a secret kiai. But you are to blame, not me," I replied.

How mysterious the secret kiai was! Was that the one reflecting the viability of our Togakure ryu ninjutsu over a thousand years? At one time or another I find myself in a dream floating in space, fully understanding the truth Takamatsu sensei's secret kiai had.

Takamatsu in China

This is a story from when Jutaro was 26 years old. In various places in China he entered martial arts contests and was never beaten. So, he was recommended to be the chairman of the Japanese Association of Young Martial Artists.

Lord Ren, the uncle to the former Emperor of China, treated Jutaro as if he were his own son. He always bragged that his Jutaro was a top-rate martial artist. This was no wonder because at this time Jutaro had more than eight hundred Chinese, Japanese, American, and French students. Every night, he taught 70–80 students. Even in the raging heat of midsummer, he did not show a drop of sweat.

Hearing these facts, a Shaolin kung fu master, Choshiryu from the Santo province, challenged Jutaro to a match. Choshityu lifted a 248-pound barbell 100 times every morning.

Jutaro refused twice but Choshiryu would not accept his refusal. That night, Jutaro dreamed of a red giant demon who swung a heavy iron bar to catch a little butterfly. The butterfly effortlessly avoided the blows time and time again. Sweat poured off the red demon and in a while he fell down and yelled, "Enough!" The next morning, Jutaro conceived the butterfly dance technique.

Lord Ren came to see Jutaro and said, "Jutaro, Choshiryu has come again. What shall we do?"

Jutaro replied, "This is the third time that he has proposed a match. This time I will accept his proposal." Lord Ren said, "Thank you, this will be a great event!" Lord Ren told everyone he passed in the city and then informed Choshiryu of Jutaro's acceptance. Choshiryu was 37 years old, weighed 248 pounds, and was approximately 1.9 meters tall. Jutaro weighed 165 pounds. The match was held in the plaza of the English settlement. With Lord Ren acting as referee, the match began with Choshiryu giving a yell and jumping 5 meters closer and kicking with the speed of a giant dragon.

Jutaro jumped to the right by 3 meters.

Choshiryu jumped up, down, right, and left within an eye's blink.

When he came again with the deadly striking hand kick, Jutaro saw an unguarded point. He tried to use the crawl position blow. Choshiryu jumped up 2 meters and returned fierce kicks and punches.

The heated battle had gone on about two hours when he noticed that Choshiryu was out of breath and was sweating profusely. His movements had clearly slowed. The weak point of a big fighter— inability to endure long battles—started to appear. Choshiryu's vision was impaired because of the sweat that ran down his face. Jutaro did not perspire a drop. When Jutaro said, "Here I come," with a calm smile on his lips, Lord Ren stopped the fight. The audience yelled for them to continue fighting. But Lord Ren could see that Choshiryu had no chance of winning.

Jutaro and Choshiryu smiled at each other in congratulations for having such a good match.

After the match, Lord Ren, Choshiryu, and Jutaro went to a restaurant to celebrate a newfound friendship, the kind that can only come from respect earned during such a competition as they had. Choshiryu praised Jutaro, while the younger man modestly returned the older man's compliments. Choshiryu announced that he wanted Jutaro to be his brother, so they sealed this martial bond with a drink of sake.

There are few ties between friends that are closer than those of brothers in martial arts.

5
Message from the Winds

I was born in Nodashi in Chiba prefecture, next to Tokyo. The day was December 2, 1931, early in the morning, just as the sun had decided to grace us with its presence for another day. Before my birth, my young mother had suffered badly and the difficult delivery stretched her courage. The midwife drew me out backwards from my mother's womb, slapped my back, held me upside down, and shook me many times. I responded to this with a slight whimper. And so I was born into the world; my first act of concealment ended, upside down looking at the ceiling.

When I first wanted to know about ninjutsu in my youth I faced the mountains that were the birthplace of ninjutsu and cried out like I was calling for a lover of whom I had lost sight. No matter how long I waited or how much I demanded the ninja to come out, there was no answer. Finally, forty years later that reply has reached my door. But when I opened the letter all I found was a blank piece of white paper. To reply to the ninja, all I could do was to pick up my pen and write for everyone to read.

Samurai displayed their power by marrying into good families, creating children ancestors of noble standing, and having a respected

53

family tree. In contrast, merchants endure by displaying their noren (goodwill) and by honorably doing business. The heritage of the ninjas for generations has been to pass on their knowledge to their apprentices. This knowledge and heritage serves as the principle in their lives. The spirit of shinobi (concealment) will aid them.

The proof that man is wind is the trace that remains after the person has left.

This "trace," this heritage, lives in my body. And like the skin of a tiger, it wraps around my body. My warrior name is "Toratsugu" (the tiger that follows). The winds of shinobi mold me. They disappear after shaping my body and leave me like a wreck on a wild ocean.

Ninja live in a protected wind. The wind runs directly into the flames, fans them, climbs to the heavens, and gathers great skills. The wind kami bestows honor and good fortune.

On my journey, searching for the roots of the ninja, I was aided by a favorable wind so that my body almost floated above the ground. This favorable wind soothed my heart. When the direction of the wind changed or the wind fanned a whirlpool, I avoided the wind, using the techniques of doton (hiding by the earth), and waited for another wind to come for me. When there was a stillness in the air, I discovered something else that was floating. This was the shinobi wind.

The shinobi wind blew continuously for two weeks in May of 1986 from San Francisco to Albuquerque. The shinobi wind allowed me to work with only an average sleeping time of two hours a night because it gave me the reincarnation of the wind kami to help transmit the spirit of shinobi. Then, not only in America but in all countries, the winds of popularity were flowing over ninjutsu—it could be likened to a ninjutsu goldrush. The people who had learned karate, kung fu, or the other martial arts, and who knew nothing of the essence of ninjutsu, profited greatly by grabbing the shinobi wind. The world was seeing karate ninja, kung fu ninja, and martial arts ninja.

There were a few people who did not catch a glance of the real ninja; they received no message from the real ninja, but because of them dangerous training accidents occurred. They dressed in ninja clothes, and crimes were committed.

They did not even know why a real ninja wears what he does. Nor did they appreciate that the black color of the ninja's costume really represents forbearance and the concealed righteousness of man. Forbearance means being able to maintain concealment no matter what insults and oppression exist.

No matter how strong or weak he may have appeared on the surface, the true ninja confronts the enemies of the spirit with a transparent suit of armor. In face of the concealed armor the wind of the enemy is carried away. The humble clothing of the ninja leader uses the thirty laws of heaven, earth and man, surface and interior, and the five techniques of hiding. With these, the ninja disappears into the wind. But when necessary he can appear together with the wind.

Dressed in humble clothes I appeared before a seminar in San Francisco and brought the message of the winds. With words and gestures from my heart, I talked to these people. I did not need their languages because I spoke with the spirit of the wind.

I spoke on the playful nature of ninjutsu. Monkeys are playful when young, but stop playing once they become adults. Man, on the other hand, has the ability to play all his life. Confucius said that people blessed with a playful heart lead the happiest lives. I emphasized the importance of playfulness. But there was more than one reason for this. If I had tried to force ninjutsu down their throats they would have reacted negatively and not listened as attentively as they did. I wanted them first to understand the ukemi or safe ways of falling down with body and spirit. I opened the gate of concealment and allowed them to feel the wind.

During the seminar someone asked me to show them a kukinage (an "air throw" or "wind technique"). So I got my assistant Ashihara to sit in a chair and I stood in front of him, my backside very close to him, and began to move as if I was going to pass wind. He held his nose and fell backward. I asked if people understood kukinage. After a pause there was great pleasure and laughter. I did not want to hurt anyone, yet I did not want my demonstrations to be artificial. If the students attending my seminar had known ukemi, we could have explored more aggressive techniques. But without the knowledge of how to fall without being hurt, they would not learn but instead be injured or afraid.

The great strategist Sun Tzu said that he who knows the enemy and knows himself shall win all the battles. The balance of the forbearing shinobi is essential at these times.

The kyojitsu tenkan ho, or the interchange of the concepts of false-hood and actuality, should apply here. Besides, there were many in the audience who understood my kukinage after watching it before. Even in an environment like the seminar it is important to keep the balance of forbearing shinobi with control.

The Otogi Pass beyond the River Hattori. It is said that Tokugawa Ieyasu crossed over the Pass led by Tarao Mitsutoshi and his son when he fled from Sakai through Ujitawara to Ise at the time of the Honnoji uprising in 1582 (when Oda Nobunaga was killed by his retainer, Akechi Mitsuhide).

The Otogi Pass: To interpret the word "Pass" as the crisis being over would lead you to a new stage of life.

The monument at the top of the Pass.

Otogi Pass overlooks the Iga Province.

The strategy and changes of taijutsu have something in common with the strategy and changes of Mother Nature.

Forgetting oneself and wanting to know only tricks and techniques, one cannot measure the balance of the wind: that is, the balance of shinobi's heart and shinobi's techniques.

In Albuquerque I became friends with a karate master. He is a warrior who, regardless of the time or place, reads the messages of the winds. He actually is receiving messages from the wind in the battlefield. This can also be likened to the presentiment of danger possessed by ninja. He has stood on the battleground and received the wind's message from behind him—pushing him forward so the bullets fly away from him. His powerful eyes reflect a beautiful light. Yet in one direction of that light there is shade. He said with conviction that there is a sharp distinction between eyes which have passed the stage of life and death, and other eyes which have not. Just at that moment his eyes shone with the glow of the moon's light. I saw that in his eyes the wind was traveling. His eyes were the receptacles that received the messages from the winds and the techniques.

Into my mailbox come messages from around the world. Later, these correspondents visit Japan. The messages are increasing year by year. After returning to their countries, these visitors continue to send me their messages. Even if there are no exchanges of letters there are still people who send me messages in spirit.

The fifteen years of correspondence between Takamatsu sensei and myself is enough to fill a bank vault. I have never in our fifteen years thrown away even one of his letters. When I read them I forget entirely about time. Whenever he remembered a secret message, he sent me a letter. He often sent me letters every three days. Reading them, I feel words appear to expand and consume the space around me. Even though I am now farsighted I can read them easily. In his writings I can see his wishes and secrets. Even now I am speaking to him and he is speaking to me through these words.

Thinking about the wind, Zen, and martial arts, I want to turn my thoughts to Buddhist monks. When some people think of Zen, that is, the practical appearance of Zen, they think of a mendicant monk. Ikkyu was a monk, blown by the wind as he rode a cloud. The cloud became his stage, but he lived in the real world. We could also call it a practice arena. He loved his mother, which may be proven by the many stories that are contained in the *Kyounshu* collection of his writings about a monk in southern Koshu in China.

The name of the monk was Bokushu. He made his living by selling various objects and lived with his mother. As a common individual he trained himself in Zen. The high level of awakening he achieved—the stage atop the clouds—must have been very moving.

From the age of seventy-seven, Ikkyu lived with a woman of unmatched beauty in a paradise existence until he died in his eighty-eighth year. The monks of those days forbade female company but he broke the rules nevertheless. You can see the natural bravery he possessed. He wrote that in the woman's most tender area, he experienced the fragrance of daffodils. He saw this as an expression of the incarnation of the Buddha.

From whom did he take lessons in breaking the rules?

The monk called Jimei was a splendid teacher, but sometimes he would break training and think entirely about having fun by embracing a woman and taking her body for his own.

Shinran, one of Japan's famous monks, also violated the ban on loving women. Rennyo had eleven wives and bore twenty-seven children. Were they giving a warning to those monks of the Tendai sect who were supposed to find sexual pleasure in young boys? It is said that this was why Shinran was married.

Why am I talking about the world of love? When men stop in an unnatural place, they go mad. There must be a balance between rules and human nature.

To read messages in a feeling of normalcy, a natural environment is needed. Messages to different worlds, and messages from different worlds—these recur when we ride on the secret shinobi winds. The messages of the winds come and go. I really believe the messages of the ninja are the messages of love.

Ri Hotei

Ri Hotei lived in the residence of a Geisha. Her personality was quiet and she was not tainted by the evil ways of the house. The way she moved and laughed was sweet and graceful and she moved the hearts of all who saw her.

She composed poems, wrote essays, and also embroidered beautifully. (In China, ladies of the gay quarters were recognized by society.) She was 18 years of age. She always grieved over her situation. But even while she led this existence of dust made to dance by the wind, she remained pure and untainted.

One day, when she was sitting in a reverie after putting on her makeup, she heard quarreling voices from outside her window. She hurriedly put on her gown and went outside. A Taoist priest and a customer had been fighting. The beaten customer lay at the bottom of the stairs. Hotei asked a familiar Shorin monk to help the customer. The Taoist priest lost to the Shorin monk and ran away with his tail between his legs.

Hotei invited the customer into her room and asked the reason for the fight. The customer answered, "He has long been my archenemy. Thank you for saving my life. To show my appreciation I would like to present you with ten pieces of silver." Saying this, he grabbed his bag with both hands, pulled out some money, and put the silver on the table.

Hotei laughed and said, "Someone who does not lend a hand to justice is a coward and one who does not save a dying man goes against the way of nature. I am not one who wants money. Do you not think of me as a human being?" She refused to take the money.

This act moved the customer's heart. He proposed to buy her and to keep her at his manor. Hotei refused, for she wanted to stay near her family grave to properly protect it. Later, she bought some land and built a manor on it. She paid a large sum of money to her foster mother (in China girls are sold at a young age and raised to adulthood). Thus, she had paid all of her debts. She also invited her relatives to live with her.

6
Ninjutsu and the Martial Arts

The ninja boom, which was triggered in the United States, has spread to Europe and is now at its height just like the gold rush in the last century. This has led to the ubiquitous appearance of would-be ninjas who, with little knowledge of ninjutsu, have tried to make easy money. So easily could they make money with their superficial knowledge and experience that they seemed intoxicated by their success. They can be likened to those good-natured men in the *Hsi Yu Chi* or *Monkey* who were swallowed up through the gourd to be turned into sake. Necessarily, some began to do wrong under the cloak of the ninja.

Thinking that something had to be done in the cause of ninjutsu, I made up my mind to fly over to the United States with eight of my students. Starting from San Francisco, we crossed over to Cleveland and then down to Albuquerque. Every seminar we had was full of enthusiasts who wanted to see with their own eyes the essentials of ninjutsu. I said to my audience, "Real ninjutsu is not for assassins or wrongdoers, but for those who wish to cultivate perseverance and endurance in order to find better ways of leading a happy life.

"The true messages I'm going to utter or demonstrate at this seminar can lead to the happiness and peace of the people of your country; therefore, a great responsibility rests upon you all."

In this world of nothingness one must see through
to the essence of common sense, or knowledge, or
consciousness; make a decision; and translate it into
action. This is the one way to enlightenment.

Let me explain what the ninja ought to know by making references to
a densho scroll explaining the purpose of the Togakure ryu ninjutsu.

Looking back over nine hundred years of history, ninjutsu was
understood as shinobu ho or a way of perseverance and endurance; and
then came to be called ninjutsu (*nin*, meaning "perseverance" or
"endurance," is the noun form of the verb *shinobu*, meaning "to
persevere" or "to endure;" and *jutsu* means "an art"). The well-tried
ninjutsu developed into ninpo, which embraces a religious and philo-
sophical concept as well as the art of war.

The Hiketsubun of the scroll tells of the importance of maintaining
the proper attitude of spirit and mind. So far as martial arts are
concerned, a wrong and biased spirit ruins one. For instance:

- The medical art is generally supposed to save one's life, whereas
  it might result in one's death should it be wrongly applied.
  (This may give you a hint for reviewing current medical
  treatments.)
- Food and drink is indispensable to one's life, whereas excessive
  eating and drinking may lead to liver or heart trouble, or other
  diseases. It is true that moderation is everything to one's
  health.
- Political leaders are expected to rule their own nation and to
  take the responsibility for the protection of their own people;
  whereas they may ruin their nation and leave their people in
  great distress should they become greedy, lacking in wisdom,
  or egocentric. Emperor Nero, the tyrant of the Roman Empire,
  is one of the worst examples of such corrupted responsibility.
- Religion, when based on sincere faith, will reveal its
  righteousness, placing individuals under the grace of God,
  bringing happiness to one's family, and doing good to the
  society. Once a religion loses its original focus, however, it
  becomes a deadly thing which can ruin individuals and even an
  entire nation.

- The martial arts can also be corrupted. Concerns can become excessively focused on rigid techniques and formalities, losing sight of their human aspects. This kind of formalism can be observed all through the history of cultural developments.

What I would like you to keep in mind here is the fact that there is a Zen wind blowing in the martial arts. Without this human spirit, no martial artist can ever attain the kanjin-kaname vital secret of ninjutsu. The kanjin-kaname is the "mind and eyes of god" (which usually reads shin-i-shingan but can also be read kanjin-kaname phonetically). A master martial artist should, through training in martial arts and ninjutsu, have a sense of human touch. Consciousness evaporated from this sense of human touch becomes the mind and eyes of god. This evaporation opens one's true eyes to happiness by placing one under the protection of god. In other words, to attain the kanjin-kaname is to comprehend heavenly justice.

This photo fades as if telling me that my present students are merely ghosts of the past—the tradition continues.

Takamatsu sensei always told me that the ninja should dedicate themselves to sincerity and justice. Sincerity is also interpreted as "trust." Trust or shin in Japanese has many meanings. It can be understood as "advent" or "coming," which may be the advent of the mind and eyes of god or communication between human beings and god. It also means "faithfulness" or "being unsuspicious." When I trained under Takamatsu sensei's guidance, doubt assailed me every once in a while. When I began to doubt I tried to stick to his teachings.

Nothing is so uncertain as one's own common sense or knowledge.

Regardless of one's fragile knowledge one must singlemindedly devote oneself to training, especially in times of doubt. It is of utmost importance to immerse and enjoy oneself in the world of nothingness. In this world of nothingness, one must see through to the essence of common sense, or knowledge, or divine consciousness, make a decision, and translate it into action. This is the one way to enlightenment. This is also the key to cultivating the sixth sense required of martial artists and ninja.

Maintaining human touch and immersing oneself in heaven simultaneously is a necessity. The five natural elements of moku (wood), ka (fire), do (earth), kin (metal), and sui (water) cannot exist without earth. Likewise, the four seasons of spring, summer, fall, and winter cannot be clearly separated without the doyo season or dog days. The four seasons without the doyo season or the five natural elements without earth are of no significance.

A person, when being righteous and sincere, is in accordance with heavenly justice. When a person attains understanding of heavenly justice, he serves the will of god. This is why I referred to the "mind and eyes of god." Therefore, the ninja is a person aware of justice.

The above-mentioned principles are the foremost requirements of the ninja. Neither the power of invisibility nor superhuman actions are the first consideration. The ninja are not members of a circus. Nor are the ninja robbers, assassins, or betrayers. The ninja are none other than persons of perseverance or endurance. Togakure-ryu ninpo is the very evidence that the ninja have lived and protected their happy lives over a thousand years.

Let me move on to my next theme: the philosophy of the martial arts. This is not my personal opinion but the teachings of the nine schools of ninjutsu. The purpose of bujutsu or martial arts is to protect nation, society, and self from harm.

Jutsu or technique is of utmost importance to all martial arts. Take kendo, or Japanese fencing, for example. Indeed, the sword is indispensable to kendo, but one cannot handle the sword exclusively with the help of physical force. Even wood-chopping requires jutsu or a technique. What puts life into jutsu is the mind.

Jutsu and the mind work together. Without right-mindedness no improvement can be expected in jutsu.

The immature mind is far from reason. Reason also goes hand in hand with jutsu. Without reason no jutsu exists in the true sense of the word.

I hope that after the ninja boom is gone with the wind, only humane people who seek the truth of ninjutsu will remain.

Even those who lay claim to being master ninja or qualified for the eighth rank should keep this philosophy in mind, because there is no obvious, material evidence of it. So subtle is this jutsu that it soon disappears when one asks for it and reappears when one is resigned to its nonexistence. This jutsu, along with the mind and reason, is the basis of martial arts.

The Hiketsubun of the densho scroll which tell what the ninja ought to know and the philosophy of martial arts were considered to be the arcana of ninjutsu. I hope you will attach great importance to the mind and eyes of ninpo or martial arts and the communication between the mind and god. As for myself, fifty years have passed since I began to follow the way of martial arts, then ninpo. Now at last I have been able to hear the chanting of each passage of the martial arts scriptures, which could be likened to the chanting of Chinese poems. The chanting washes off the dirt of our minds as if it were the sound of a koto or Japanese harp played by a heavenly maiden. This is why I have presented to you the philosophy of martial arts as faithfully as I can without adding my own interpretations to what I was taught by my master.

"Strong" and "weak" are common words on martial artist's lips. However, I make it a rule to advise my pupils that they should behave as squarely as possible, doing what the ninja ought to do. After all, a man must be a hero to understand a hero. I advise my pupils to try not to overcome the enemy but to become men who can live. The movements of ninpo taijutsu are not supposed to be seen as "strong" or "weak," but rather movements that bring one un or fortune.

Thus you must find the truth of ninpo taijutsu that brings you un or opportunities. It is just like a dragon calls forth a cloud (also pronounced "un" in Japanese). When a dragon calls forth a cloud, it also causes a rainfall. There is an expression "sweet rainwater" in Buddhism. Buddhists believe that taking a sip of this sweet rainwater makes one immortal. Similarly, a ninja's interpretation of the dragon's rainwater could be understood as the godsent water which confers immortality.

I am very pleased to see the current alluring ninja boom fading away.

I don't want to see my disciples deviate unconsciously from the way of ninpo and be caught in a trap of desire. I hope that after the ninja boom is gone with the wind, only the humane people who seek the truth of ninjutsu will remain. I also hope that from these true seekers one truly skillful ninja or martial artist after another will emerge and do good for the world community. I appeal to those schemers who exploit the ninja boom for their own gain that they not risk the balance of living creatures.

Neither martial artist nor ninja like fighting or violence. Ninja in the true sense of the word are artists who love the beauties of nature and the human spirit. Takamatsu sensei used to be devoted to drawings and poems. He was loved and respected by many people. I remember the words on the lips of many visitors on the day of his death, April 2, 1972, "Did Takamatsu sensei really pass away? I can't believe it." We all believed that Takamatsu sensei was a phoenix. On that day I broke a pledge of temperance for the first time in fifteen years and took a sip of okiyome (sake served at funeral services in Japan). For the fifteen years I trained under Takamatsu sensei's guidance, Mrs. Takamatsu used to serve me dinner with two bottles of sake. I refused, however, to taste sake, as I thought that I should not take the liberty of drinking while learning under Takamatsu sensei. I often wish we had drunk together, seeing his smiles. But all I could do in those days was train under his guidance.

On our way home from our visit to Takamatsu sensei's tomb in the sixteenth year after his death, Takamatsu's daughter and I talked together, seeing the full-blown cherry blossoms through the windows. She said, "Whenever Dad heard of your coming, he didn't even notice the cherry blossoms, just walked to-and-fro in the house, waiting for your visit. How delighted he must have been to have you as a student!" She then added, "Now you are the only disciple that Dad has left." She uttered these words cheerlessly as if she were talking to the hazy cherry blossoms.

"I will follow his teachings as long as I live," I murmured toward the heavens high above the cherry blossoms.

Now I remember Takamatsu sensei's words ringing in my ears, "I'm not telling you to defeat the enemy, but be a man who can live. Never be enslaved by martial arts—take pleasure in them. I wonder if only one out of tens of thousands of people can take pleasure in martial arts, though."

Yonindori

While attending Akashi no Miya's English school, Jutaro also attended the Chinese Literature institute. Every other day, he practiced at the dojo of Mizuta Yoshitaro Tadafusa sensei to learn the Takagi Yoshin ryu style jujutsu. He also went from time to time to Toda Shinryuken's dojo to learn the secrets of Togakure ryu ninjutsu.

One Sunday evening, Jutaro was strolling in the amusement park by the seashore when he saw two children, one about 8 and the other about 12 or 13, fighting over a swing. Four men appeared and started to root for the older child. Strengthened by the support, the older child hit the younger one. The smaller one hurled himself at his opponent who fell down face up and the smaller boy saddled him like a horse.

At that moment, one of the men hit the smaller boy. Jutaro cried out that an adult should not hit a child. He went forward to help the child when two of the four men came and grabbed Jutaro's arms. One moved behind him and squeezed his middle. The last of the four moved in front of him, grabbed his collar, and started to kick him. Jutaro gave a kiai, and in a blink of an eye, he had thrown all four of them into the river which flowed behind him.

I later heard that the big men who had grabbed Jutaro's arms were sumo wrestlers of the Juryo rank. The one who grabbed him from behind was nicknamed the demon of Okuratani village and was a licensed instructor of Ishizaki sensei's Takagi yoshin ryu. The one who grabbed his collar was a man famed for having the strength of five men. With his iron-like body, he could easily carry a 165-pound rock up the 108 stone steps of Hitomaru shrine. No one could deal with these men even if they were to fight them one at a time. News of Jutaro's victory became known and it was said that a great demon had appeared.

7
Taijutsu:
Form and Spirit

Once one reaches a high level in taijutsu technique, just a slight difference in movements often decides victory or defeat. Even if the motion is almost perfect—with one small mistake—it sometimes becomes a matter of life and death.

There is an old saying, "If a mouse gets cornered, he might even bite a cat." It is true; people will unexpectedly do something beyond their strength when they are in real peril. This proverb is reminiscent of a taijutsu method: that is, you step back as if you were withdrawing from your opponent but actually you are holding him to you.

During taijutsu practice, my trainees often say to me, "I am sometimes sure that I have you cornered; in fact, however, you catch me before I know it." It is not that I dodge him at the last moment, as is generally believed; rather, I hold his whole body and soul as if I were wrapping him up in my life itself.

There is a Taijutsu book titled *The Feats of Cats*, in which an old cat and a young cat talk about the core of martial arts. A cat can predict the weather, see things in the darkness, walk noiselessly, let his game run away from him, and drive it into a corner to catch it there.

The late grandmaster Takamatsu often mentioned winning and

71

During taijutsu practice, my trainees often say to me, "I am sometimes sure that I have you cornered; in fact, however, you catch me before I know it." It is not that I dodge him at the last moment, as is generally believed; rather, I hold his whole body and soul as if I were wrapping him up in my life itself.

losing in nature, saying, "What does 'victory' really mean? I would never have mastered taijutsu if I had clung to that concept." Nothing is better in learning taijutsu than to give up the shallow concept of victory and defeat and to find the right way to live.

There are eight basic forms in taijutsu. Eight is considered to be a lucky number in Japan, but because the number eight "8" looks like infinity (∞), I would rather say that this "8" represents infinity and eternity. I remember it as if it were only yesterday, when the late master Takamatsu told me how important these eight basic forms were. Since then, I have stuck to them for more than twenty years. His emphasis on these eight forms is supported by Confucius's revolutionary remark: "Enjoying the arts with perfect virture is one of the most noble, profound acts of human beings." And through training in these eight forms over twenty years, I have learned more about life itself than self-discipline.

The eight forms are the core of taijutsu, through which we can find a way to enjoy the art itself, health, peace, and happiness. And when you finally reach the core of the art, you will know what a performance in emptiness could really mean.

We say in Japanese that a presentiment is "a message conveyed by an insect." For example, when someone is dying, his family, or close friends he really loved, can feel that something is happening. We say that an insect has conveyed a message to them. It makes us believe that one can communicate through the subconscious. Many have actually escaped from danger owing to this so-called sixth sense.

Remembering how passionately grandmaster Takamatsu told me these stories comparing a man to an insect, I close my eyes: I then see a firefly drawing a curve with his glowing tail. The curve is gradually shaping into a circle. An invisible insect in the invisible circle talks to me.

I am sometimes asked; "What should we do if we get lost in life?"

The answer is quite simple. "Think nothing and follow your subconscious."

"How should we prepare ourselves when we are in a real fight?" asked my students.

I often reply, "You don't need religion, you don't need philosophy, you don't need culture, either, as they often rule you. But I say that the bigger capacity you have in yourself, the more you can accept."

"What do you mean by capacity?" they ask.

"Power that works even when you don't have any power in you."

Act as intuition dictates and you will see the secrets of taijutsu there.

Guns and the Ninja

About 100 years after guns were intoduced to Japan by the Portuguese in 1543, they became less popular. Some people say that this was due to the era of peace which resulted from Tokugawa Ieyasu's takeover of the entire country. Others say that the highest-ranking warriors were too proud to take up guns because of the opinion that guns were for cowards. Such weapons were usually given to those warriors at the bottom of the hierarchy. Still another view is that people began to give artistic value to guns by engraving decorative designs, no longer making them tools of combat, but collector's items. Some people cite sakoku, or the fact that the country was closed to foreigners.

Sodezutsu or sodeteppo a hand-held small cannon or gun. This is a bamboo gun laminated with nine sheets of paper.

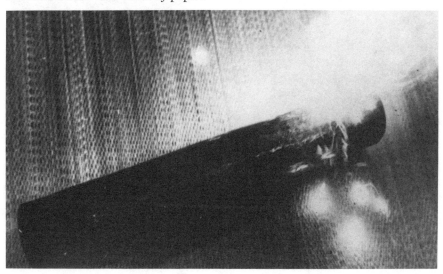

Ninja also have used guns. If I say that they somehow obtained guns, then I believe many people may get the wrong impression. According to historical records, the ninja used wooden cannons, made by hollowing out a tree trunk and reinforcing the wood by laminating it with paper. These cannons were carried in one's arms. Another type was made by laminating bamboo with Japanese paper and filling the hollow center with gunpowder and bullets. These long "rifles" were about the length of one's sleeve and each had a fuse. Such guns were not very accurate.

Takamatsu sensei told me the following story when he passed on to me the techniques of using such sleeve guns:

> A warrior named Sanada Yukimura stole into Ieyasu's camp in Mt. Chausu. He fired a sleeve gun at Ieyasu, but missed. This episode is recorded in a chapter of *Yurushimono Goki*. It is said that ninja knew how to use gunpowder even before guns were imported to Japan and that it enhanced their skills of Katon no jutsu. They used throwing blades with gunpowder wrapped around them, or fire arrows, bamboo mortars, and grenades in place of guns.

The sodeteppo in use.

I should explain here about weapons and fighting. When I am teaching a large number of pupils, I begin with taijutsu which is then followed by a transition period when I let them take up weapons. What is interesting is that the pupil's character and whether he has mastered the taijutsu become self-evident when he is allowed to work with weapons.

I have practiced shooting and I am quite successful. The instructors are surprised by my skills and ask me if I have had much experience in using pistols and I tell them that I haven't. The question, then, is how I can be so accurate, and I believe it can be explained by the fact that I am well-trained in taijutsu. The wonderful thing about taijutsu is that it will greatly help you in handling weapons that you have never used before.

Nageteppo or throwing guns.

You may have experienced aiming your gun at a bird. At such a moment, you can see that a bird's instincts are well-developed. If you aim an unloaded gun at the bird or if you have no intention to shoot, the bird does not fly away. Shinkengata or real combat taijutsu allows you to develp consciousness like that of the bird or wild animals. But I would like you to realize that such training will allows you to possess splendid techniques because you have already developed a human consciousness.

Sometimes I am asked to train policeman on how to use guns and how to take a pistol away from an approaching criminal. I am asked what to do in a situation where you are about three meters away from the culprit and, consequently, he is out of reach. I can't answer that question. There are probably many areas and movements that I cannot answer with my knowledge of taijutsu. What is unknown is answered by the visionary taijutsu.

Matchlock guns.

Ohzutsu or wooden mortar.

The ninja are not members of a circus. Nor are the ninja robbers or assassins or betrayers. The ninja are none other than persons of perseverance or endurance.

Chan Lee Soo was a magician who let someone from the audience shoot a loaded gun at him and caught the bullet between his teeth. One day, the screw of his musket had gotten old, and the ammunition ignited during one of his shows, accidentally firing a bullet. The bullet pierced his right lung and Lee died a tragic death. The most amazing speed cannot always stop a bullet.

A difference in sensitivity is proven here. I have already spoken about ninjutsu as being the art of escape, of fleeing, or of avoidance. The ninja used his skills to avoid being hit by the bullets fired from guns but also to avoid confrontation if that was the wisest decision. That is how my ryu or school has continued to exist for 900 years.

Those of us who practice the art of stealth desire to live peaceful lives without guns. When people say that guns are used in the game of give-and-take, then living creatures are killed and lives lost. We say it is a game of give-and-return—those who shoot will have their fire returned.

This is the same with the martial arts today. The martial arts, judo and kendo, practiced today were all developed after the Meiji Period to be enjoyed as sports. However, I get the strange feeling that they are too oriented toward actual fighting, yet not sufficient. The martial accomplishments of my nine schools have survived over a thousand years of being in the midst of actual fighting. Therefore, it is possible to immediately get a feel for actual combat.

From the right-hand guard posture (like an old person with a stick), the opponent attacks with katate buri (one hand swing). Use nayashi (soft blocking) against the attack.

Hold opponent's stick to your body with your left elbow. Opponent is then trapped with omote gyaku onikudaki gata.

My body flow (NAGARE) with the lower body moving toward opponent makes him roll.

You will see applications in muto sabaki (unarmed technique against sword attack) through studying the following stick technique.

*By just lowering my body, the opponent is
unbalanced and feels pain in his elbow.*

Stop moving when your opponent stops.

Motions in the pictures have two
faces which are falsehood and
actuality (kyo-jitsu). These may also
be called commonsense and nonsense.
However, if someone misuses this
kyo-jitsu concept, which should only
be a mutation in the right
direction, one must know that death
is waiting for him.

Bisento jutsu

The basic method against a long weapon is still the same as previous technique. "Move like wind in the opponent's empty space."

Watch the attacking flow of the opponent.

Use the big momentum of the long weapon. Spin him like a top so that the vortex motion threatens opponent's eyes (metsubushi).

Rokushaku bo

Move forward against any long weapon attack (swing, stab, or hit).

Opponent falls down on the stick, his right arm often twisted.

Slowly *and naturally drop your own body.*

Using leverage, throw him by taking advantage of opponent's pulling-back motion.

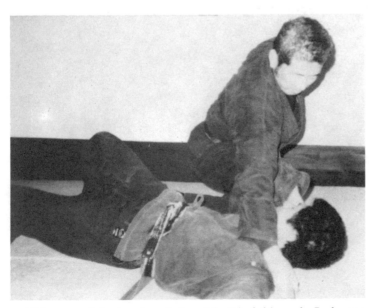

Using my right hand and the stick, I lock his neck. I also use my right knee to pin his body.

Mutodori (Hekiku)—Unarmed

*Against your opponent's downward slash,
push up against the pommel.*

Finishing: pinning opponent's hand.

Or jump in and kick.

Continue to move in and grab the sword behind his head, then drop his body down to the mat.

Or sudden counter-attack to the head using opponent's sword.

Mutofuten (Muto Chokkengata)—Straight style

First, the essence of Mutodori *is to realize that the secret spot is just one step in front of you.*

Step forward like the wind.

Put your left elbow slightly on opponent's right arm.

Stepping in with the right timing is a key.

*Do not move against the opponent's motion. Just move as if you are a gentle wind. This should apply to any angle—right-left, forward-rear, up-down (*taihenjutsu*).*

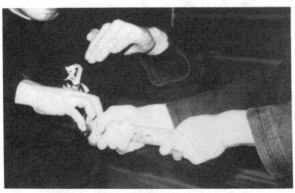

Hold sword guard with your third and fourth fingers of right hand then chop down with the left.

Rakurai struck by a thunderbolt.

Tengoku Mutogaeshi

The opponent is trying to attack my left leg or left body. It is not necessary to move.

My left hand also holds the hilt. Putting the blade upward as in omote gyaku.

When the attack comes to me, I make a big step toward front. The opponent's attack flows through empty air and I pivot in next to him.

With taihen jutsu (gyokko-style), my right hand holds the hilt.

Then, attack opponent's neck.

Placing my right hand on the back of the blade, I cut his neck.

The opponent is in his attacking posture (hasso no kamae).

Yama Arashi
(Mountain Storm)

Twisting in, my right hand attacks his left hand. I can use any fist attack with my right hand. Note that the body movement (flow) is important. Disarm opponent while he falls, trying to escape from his arm pain.

Unarmed technique against the attack (shiraha dori). I dive in, my left hand holding the bottom of his left arm.

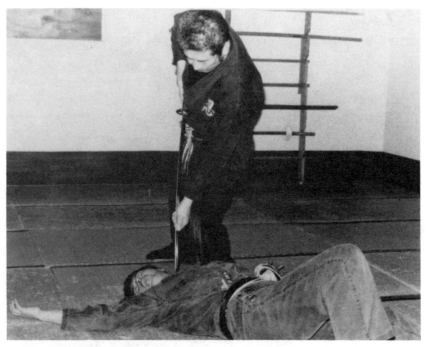

The finish—the mountain collapses after the storm.

Opponent is in his attacking posture—fall tinted leaves.

Maiyou (Dancing leaves)

Then, I dance like a leaf in the wind too.

Opponent's attack—Winter blasts and the dancing leaves sweep down.

Move forward and hold opponent's arms.

Continued on page 94.

Maiyou (Dancing leaves)

Continued from page 93.

(Taihen jutsu) Pivot, and drive him down-like overturning leaves.

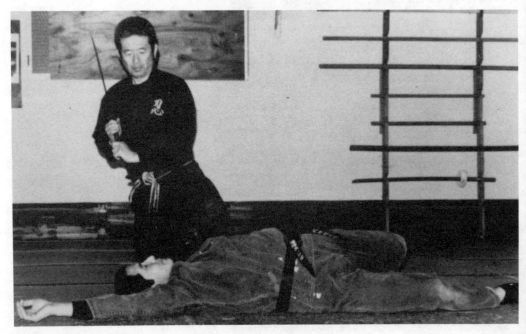

Kneeling posture—hold the sword like a standing tree.

The opponent falls—fallen leaves—and naturally the sword can be released.

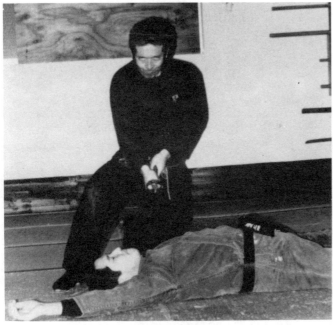

Finishing—like a winter blast.

Your opponent is in seigan no kamae.

Hatou—Wave motion

Hit freely with your right hand. Then make his body float up in the air with your left hand.

Moving forward, hold your opponent's left arm with your left hand.

Hit at his face with your right hand.

Continued on page 98.

Continued from page 97.

Then hit opponent's right upper arm with a shuto.

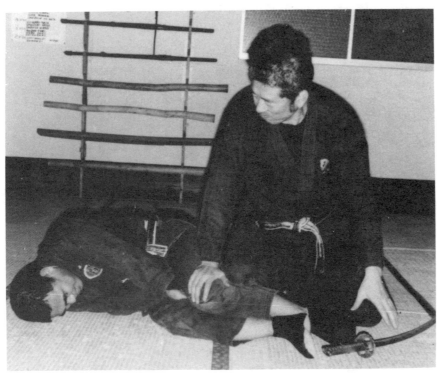

Sweep opponent's leg with your right foot and then you have choices for finishing.

Hiten—Jump and Roll

Natural posture against opponent's seiga no-kamae.

Dive in.

Put your hand under opponent attacking hands with sanslin-gata-taihen.

And roll.

Continued on page 102.

Continued from page 101.

Both opponent's arms are reversed and in pain, and he releases the sword. (Detail from other side.)

Raise to kneeing posture with taihen.

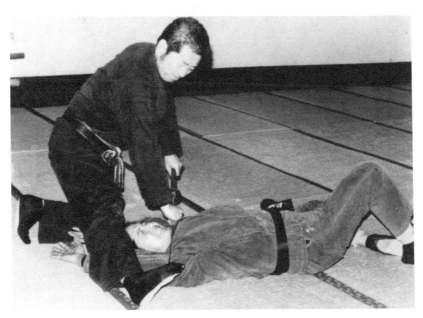

Take his sword and counterattack.

Assume a gyokko ryu hanin no kamae against opponent's chudan-no-kamae.

Suiryu—water flow

I drive his body down so the sword is now under my control.

I dive in with Hanin. My left hand controls his right hand, and my right hand holds the back of the blade.

Using my body, I push the sword while pulling his right arm with my left hand.

Naturally, take the sword.

*I stand in doko no kamae against oppo-
nent's kasumi no kamae.*

Doko (angry tiger)

*I attack his right upper arm with my left
elbow. If opponent moves then any left
hand strike is useful. Hold the back of the
blade with both hands (shiraha dori).*

*I lock his arms with my underarm, then
twist my body to turn over the blade and
put it on his neck.*

He thrusts, and with my left sanshin
strike, I move into opponent's right side.

Pulling off my body from him, I lock his
neck with my left elbow and the sword.

Finish.

Opponent's tenchi no kamae.

MOKO—wild tiger

My left knee is also freely working to unbalance my opponent. (Detail.)

I block the attack with my left hand and elbow—showing as a tiger displays its claws to its enemy.

Shiraha dori action centers on my left elbow. Normally, Muto-dori technique is not just hand technique—it is controlled with the elbow.

Turn over the blade—toragaeshi.

Stab with wild tiger's fang.

Tenchosetsu

The Emperor's birthday came on the eleventh. Matatago, a contrac-
tor, was in charge of decorating the Japanese settlement. Jutaro
employed foreigners to decorate the roads where the streetcars passed.
His friend, Ogasawara, also used foreigners to decorate the rooftop of
the consulate. But at noon, when Jutaro called, asking Ogasawara,
who was supposed to be on the roof top, there was no answer. So, he
climbed up the ladder to see what had happened. When he got to the
roof, he saw that his friend had been beaten up by the laborers and a
few of them were about to throw him off the roof.

Jutaro jumped in front of Ogasawara to protect him. Just then, a
man came at him with a right-hand blow. Jutaro's leg flew to block
the punch. Another man punched, but Jutaro did not attack: he just
blocked the blows of his opponents. More than ten laborers fell from
the roof with no effort from Jutaro. Jutaro's fellow workers saw what
had happened and congratulated Jutaro for getting out of such a
dangerous position.

Takamatsu sensei often said, "For taijutsu, the flexibility of the
legs is the most important factor, not the strength of the legs."

110

8
The Rules of the Ninja

When I try to find the reason for the survival of the nine traditions of ninjutsu for over one thousand years, I believe it is because each soke or head of the family has passed down each experience of enlightenment by word of mouth. The family heads risked their lives in order to attain enlightenment and these experiences became the rules of the ninja.

The ninja created rules to abide by in order to obtain divine wings. These rules are naturally created and can adapt to the current of the time and environmental situation. Through them, one becomes conscious of kyojitsu tenkan ho, or properly interchanging truth and falsehood through training in ninpo taijutsu. These rules are like the seven-ways-three-directions of the ninja's method of disguise; the seven secrets of disguise plus three equals ten. Ten symbolizes a lucky charm that does away with evil.

The objectives of the ninja are: first, to use ninjutsu to infiltrate the enemy's camp and observe the situation. Then strategies for a surprise attack or internal strife can be developed. It is true we have no choice but to strive for victory in the event that our enemy takes certain actions against us, but normally we should efface ourselves in order to bring our actions to a successful conclusion. Here, I speak of the enemy

111

country as something with form, but I would like to point out that the enemy can also be found in nature or in the souls of other human beings. Furthermore, this effort should be for one's sovereign and country, to protect one's country and oneself, and to ensure peace for both sides.

Second, the ninja should work for sovereign and country through a spirit of justice, and cultivate his soul for teacher and parents. He must not use ninjutsu for his personal profit, desire, or for the purpose of entertainment.

One important point to remember in one's fight for the protection of justice is to think simply about the fact that the enemy's justice is often wrongly interpreted as not being justice.

We are told to render our services to teachers and parents. In Japan, it is said that the relationship between parent and child lasts one generation, husband and wife two generations, and that between teacher and pupil lasts three. This emphasizes how much we are indebted to our teachers and how important it is to offer our services to them.

I would like to speak about myself today, fifteen years after the death of Takamatsu sensei. My pupils have matured and I feel that I can now truly call them pupils. There is a Japanese proverb which tells us to walk one meter behind our teacher, being careful not to step on his shadow. At one time I believed that this proverb taught us to follow in our teacher's footsteps, but to keep a distance to avoid rudely stepping on his shadow. But in reality, we cannot really step on someone's shadow because the shadow is always on top of the foot which has supposedly stepped on it. A teacher is like the shadow of his pupil as well as a copy of his mentor's shadow.

On many occasions when I was taught by Takamatsu sensei I had the feeling that I would be stepping on his shadow throughout my life. But I have come to think deeply that I was not actually stepping on his shadow. Many pupils come to visit me. Some people find joy in gaining more pupils, but I do not. This is because no matter how many pupils I have, if the spirit inside me is not transmitted properly, it's the same as if I didn't have any pupils.

Even if you continue spiritual training throughout your entire life, what you can attain through spiritual awakening (as opposed to enlightenment) is limited. It's appropriate to say that what you gain is only the tip of the iceberg. What I mean is that even if you see the word for "air" that doesn't mean that you understand what air is. There are many people who cannot be spiritually awakened even if they continue this effort throughout their lives. In addition, some people are aware of the fact that they will not be able to attain enlightenment even if they continue their effort for a lifetime.

Spiritual awakening has no relationship to the amount of time one spends in training. A training hall in Buddhist terms is a place where Shakyamuni attained Buddhahood. The training hall is not a plot of land or location, it is a space for enlightenment.

There was a famous Japanese monk named Ryokan. He always played with children and one time, when bamboo shoots started growing under his house, he drilled holes in the floor to let them grow. It is said that he even drilled holes in the ceiling when the bamboo became taller. The holes eventually caused his house to collapse. Ryokan never had a training hall or pupils at any point in his life.

There was another Buddhist priest named Tosui who had a large training hall and many pupils. However, it is said he abandoned his training hall and became a beggar. He joined the masses and passed on his teachings in the streets.

I believe both Ryokan and Tosui recognized that people will flock to a training hall when it is established and that such an organization will grow; yet attendance does not assure awakening.

One is not allowed to use ninjutsu for purposes of entertainment or to perform magic. If one uses ninjutsu for such purposes, it is no longer ninjutsu but has a taint of sorcery or witchcraft. Such a performer will not be able to live in a society where he is exposed to others, but will have to live among the snakes, toads, and slugs in a world where the sun never shines.

Consciousness that arises from self-interest and selfish desire sends you in a direction with no focus. If you forget the rules of the ninja and hop on the streetcar named desire, you will arrive at the Station of the

Crook as your final destination, or Prison Station, or Coffin Station if you board the streetcar with violent thoughts in mind.

There is something peculiarly fascinating about ninjutsu. A bad

ninja who takes advantage of what he has mastered will disappear as a vulgar merchant or as a stupid gangster. Just as the followers begin to become lazy after the training hall is firmly established, when a ninja expresses his desires in a visible manner, his skills become impotent.

Third, ninjutsu places great importance on hojutsu, which is kyojitsu tenkan ho, or the method of interchanging truth and falsehood. Without revealing yourself to the enemy, you may use taijutsu, but when left no other choice, you may use happo hiken or the eight methods of using secret swords or ninja tools to confuse your enemy.

It is important to confuse him. It is possible to say that hojutsu puts more emphasis on attacking the mind than attacking the body. This means the ninja uses techniques of investigation, spying, stealth, and plotting as well as truth and falsehood to lead his community to victory.

I always tell my pupils to try to attain enlightenment through taijutsu or bodily techniques. The strategy and changes of such bodily techniques have something in common with the strategy and changes of Mother Nature. You cannot understand this unless you study under me. Training in body techniques, change, and truth and falsehood will lead you on the road of justice.

Fourth, ninja must master the use of gunpowder, ninja tools, and drugs—including good medicines as well as poisonous drugs. There is an important corollary to this rule that says you must not kill your enemy. The ninja recognize the principle that the bad end up destroying themselves. And with regard to human life, a person is considered dead if his soul is dead, although his body may still be alive. The ninja have fostered this spirit of justice.

Fifth, the ninja should spend considerable time in practicing with each of the weapons he will use. It is written that he should take advantage of and learn from his instincts. The way of handling weapons changes with the times, and what is valid today may not be valid tomorrow. In the Japanese language, *weapon* and *nothingness* are both pronounced "bu" which means that we must foster the ability to use weapons, which we have never encountered before through practice. When I visited New York, some of my companions there were amazed at how I was able to handle every weapon given to me. They called me a magician.

Sixth, the ninja must always come into direct contact with meteorology, physiography, and geography. Through meteorology and physiography, we can learn about the changes and true character of Mother

The rules of the ninja are not cruel or overly demanding. They are merely rules for the expert of stealth to follow in order to discover and protect the truth.

Nature. This is not a kind of academic learning, but actual experience. This experience involves our whole body, and we can come to understand the silent language of Mother Nature through the transmission of feelings and perception. It can be likened to conversing with god.

Seventh, at a time when Japan was at civil war, ninja who threw the rules into disorder or who broke the rules were severely punished. Even close relatives would be beheaded, exiled, or ostracized. When a war escalates, ninja are always put in a tragic situation where they must live within the confines of these rules. That is why they have a philosophy which says try to avoid fighting, and steal away and flee until the very end.

Let me explain here the meaning of the word *expulsion*. In Buddhist terms, it means to take away the rights of the follower and to expel him from that sect. In ninjutsu, it also means to dismiss a person from the ryu. But I would like to say that my interpretation is somewhat different. Rather than dismissing a pupil, I hope that he will become greatly successful through a new feeling of resolve that may result from his mistakes. So far, I have not had to expel a single pupil.

I have given up on some students. You may ask why I give up on them but not expel them. That is because they have become baser even than animals. I tell my pupils that I believe it is good not only for pupils to disagree and argue among themselves, but for masters and pupils to disagree from time to time. That doesn't mean that they should continue to hold grudges against each other. Parents and children, brothers and sisters, all of them sometimes quarrel and this is very similar. It is natural to welcome back anyone who has left the training hall but decides to return, with the same love and happiness that we would share with a family member who had run away but comes home.

Eighth, ninja must not kill others, injure honest citizens, or steal money and valuables. This is where the difference between magic and ninjutsu lies.

Ninth, the ninja must always take care of himself, build a strong body, be swift in action, and study many things as well as master many skills. I love music, play the steel guitar, perform Japanese dances; I love to write and paint, and I am working hard to develop the soul of ninjutsu.

Tenth, ninja must carry out the assigned training. There are eighteen areas of training—spiritual development, koshijutsu, koppojutsu, sword handling, stick and staff handling, blade-throwing, the use of chain and sickle, spears and halberds, horsemanship, swimming, making gunpowder, plotting, spying, trespassing, escaping, disguise, meteorology, and physiography.

The ninja is expected to train intensively. This means that one must persevere in his pursuit of this training. The life of a ninja is a simple and regular one in which he trains in all of these eighteen skills day in and day out and abides by the other rules of the ninja. These are the basic elements of the great secret of the ninja. The great secret can also be called a subtle secret. The rules of the ninja are not cruel or overly demanding. They are merely rules for the expert of stealth to follow in order to discover and protect the truth.

Let me say a few words about protective charms. No one has the upper hand in martial arts. There is a rule which teaches that the arts are techniques for defending yourself but not for attacking. This posture of defense is like a counterpunch which is stronger than an offensive punch. A person on the defensive side is more relaxed in his pose. If you have endurance and carefully plan your defense, the path to victory will naturally appear before you. It means that the god of nature will give you a protective charm. So the rules of the ninja are in fact like a charm to protect your life.

Yo Gyokko

Yo Gyokko, from Suikai, was famous throughout the land for his kenshi no jutsu (a method using the fists, fingers, and head). When he faced challengers, he sometimes killed them. There were many people who held a grudge against him, but because of his strength, there was no way to get back at him. Yo's shop prospered more and more. One day a priest came to Yo's gate and said, "The Elder at Goheiji temple has been hearing of your fame and he has sent me to request your presence." Yo casually resisted at first. But the repeated invitations convinced him of their enthusiasm. And so he decided to go. Yo's child Kaibu also went along.

The guide priest who lead the two to the temple went to report their arrival. After this, a mysterious old man of strange physical appearance, accompanied by several tens of attendants came to greet them. Kaibu could feel that these men were of evil heart and told his father to be careful. Yo replied that the priest had shown him goodwill, and besides what reason had he for fearing the priest. Yo entered the main hall. The elder priest came with his pupils and greeted Yo very respectfully. Everyone called Yo, roshi (teacher, sensei). He was very pleased to hear this. The elder invited Yo to come up to the second floor to eat and drink.

Kaibu asked, "Why does the party have to be held on the second floor. Why not on the first?"

The priest replied, "I feel your son suspects us of planning some trick. If this is so, we shall have the party on the first floor."

Yo always valued bravery and did not act by logic. And so he went upstairs. The elder said, "Yo sensei meets people with unprejudiced faith and his son is very thoughtful. Both are qualities to be respected." Everyone said celebrated words and drank.

During the drinking party, they came to the topic of martial arts. They all were in agreement. But suddenly when the bell sounded, the elder and his disciples attacked Yo with swords drawn. Yo used his fingers and head to fight against them. Fourteen priests lay dead, countless others were badly injured. Yo was also injured in a few places. Kaibu saw his father about to go after the elder. The priest, knowing that he was no match for Yo, hid behind the gate to wait for an opportune time. When Yo came near, the elder jumped out and swung at Yo's head with his sword but the head was so hard that the sword bounced off.

After this episode, Yo increased his fame in the land by killing a huge lion with only one fist. People started to call him Koto-ou (lion-battling king). It is not known how he died.

9
Ancient Legend—
Modern Spirit

The history of ninpo dates back hundreds of years. Its secrets were passed from ninja to ninja. However, the most important thing is how to venture into the unknown and finally discover the ultimate way of life through ninjutsu. Quoted here is a story told by the late grandmaster Takamatsu, which points to this ultimate way.

Deep in a rock cave on Mt. Takao in Iga province a white-haired old man with piercing eyes is sitting with a scroll in one hand. He looks like a creature from another world. In front of him, two young men, their heads down, sit like motionless rocks. The old man speaks passionately as if his voice were crushing the two rocks.

"In the first year of the Konyu era, when I was in the Ka, I lost a battle against king Jinso and fled the Shikou country—China.

"Listen. Before we started the war with Jinso, I advised the kings of Kittan and Ka that we should not have a war with king Jinso, as there would be no point in it and we were at a great disadvantage. But they never listened to me. I joined the war from my loyalty to our king, but it ended in our defeat.

"I narrowly escaped and came to Japan. The purpose of my living near the Ise Shrine, and teaching you all those things is to have you develop the right spirit for martial arts—for Japan and for the Japanese people.

"It will be disastrous if the samurai misunderstand and misuse the spirit of martial arts—people would be forced to lead miserable lives."

For an example, the old man pointed to the founder of the T'ang Dynasty (618-906 A.D.), who assembled a large army from his people. The war started in February and ended in July. A great number of people starved to death. Only three years later, the war started again. People were forcibly expelled and further thousands of them died of starvation.

The old man continued, "You should train yourselves in martial arts, at the same time keeping loyalty to your king and parents in mind, and be always ready to repay obligations. Prosperity exists only in a peaceful life. Any war or battle always results in destruction and collapse. People will learn that harmony comes first in martial arts only after they realize what war is like, how miserable its results can be.

"If the sword is used with an evil mind, it will be a murder weapon and swordsmanship will be mere killing technique. The sword is the spirit of the swordsman. It is the most disgraceful thing in swordsmanship to use the sword as a mere weapon.

"Swordsmanship is only one example. In China, Japan, or any place in the world, no martial art exists for the purpose of killing others. There is no excuse for murder in any martial art.

"Even if I told you this a hundred times, even if you two finally master all the secrets of swordsmanship, this simple truth could not be taught to you."

Indeed, I can now see great significance in his last remark, "Even if you finally master all the secrets, this simple truth cannot be taught." I can finally see the importance in these stories after thirty years of practicing.

One of the old man's two young followers, Ryutaro, later became a great master of ninjutsu named Yaryudoshi. The other one, Dosan, also overcame many difficulties, struggled for peace in his country, and was respected by people all his life under the name of Tendo Sakagami.

The old man, Hogenbo, possessed three most precious attributes. The first one was swordsmanship that can work with anyone in any place at any time, and further, that works without using a sword at all. The second one was a mirror of the mind through which everything became clear. And the third treasure he had was a good, pure spirit that brightened people around him and lived long in people's hearts even after his death. Some people believe I lead a superhuman life in which nothing is impossible. So they ask what is the secret for such a life? To this I answer: "I have been engaged in ninpo—a thousand years of history. My life is just a demonstration of its greatness."

Whenever I face difficulties, I am struck with admiration for the way that ninpo has survived all the trials and hardships through the years. There are five precepts for ninja that are quite simple but most significant to me. When I am sad, unhappy, sick, injured, or desperate, I always encourage myself by remembering them.

First, forget your sadness, anger, grudges, and hatred. Let them pass like smoke caught in a breeze. Do not indulge yourself in such feelings.

Second, you should not deviate from the path of righteousness; you should lead a life worthy of man. This simple philosophy is exactly what hundreds of sages have repeated throughout the ages. Some people believe that I am a great man. But I always tell them that I am just an ordinary man. Presence of mind consists in a very simple life, not a special or great life—I am recently confident of that.

Third, don't be possessed by greed, luxury, or your ego. If you learn martial arts purely for self-interest and always try to depend on someone else just because it is easier, you will be controlled by these three desires—even if you have already reached a high level in the martial arts. These three desires will distort not only martial arts but humanity itself.

When people are dying, there are two directions toward death: joy and suffering. Joy here means in a heavenly sense, and does not include pleasures or pastimes. Once this stage in life is reached, one will know one's real mission in life.

Fourth, you should accept sorrows, sadness, or hatred as they are and consider them a chance for trial given by the Almighty. It is the most noble spirit in ninpo to take everything as a blessing given by Nature. When you are trying to carry through something, your goodwill is sometimes considered malicious by some people who are obsessed by their own egotism. They might throw a stone at you. I try to interpret that as a blessing stone thrown to me by God for my own sake. Even Nichiren, a great Buddhist priest, was stoned by the people during his advocacy in various cities.

Fifth, have both your time and mind fully engaged in budo and have your mind deeply set on bujutsu. Read between the lines in the late grandmaster Takamatsu's story of the ninja mentioned earlier, and you will learn the attitudes and methods one should keep in ninjutsu training.

If one mistakes spiritual enlightenment for self-satisfaction, one unconsciously starts adhering to one's desires, playing by turns the

In the battle of Tensho Iga (1582 A.D.), when ninja Momochi Sandayu was attacked by Oda Nobunaga's army, he and his men were routed to Sanbonmatsu. There he told his men that there would be no more danger of being attacked. But his men did not agree. He repeated his conviction and later on that day, what he said was proved when Nobunaga was killed by his right-hand man, Akechi Mitsuhide.

Momochi Tanbanokami's grave.

The picture shows the place where Momo-chi's castle used to exist.

The graves of the Momochi families.

parts of a beast and human being in life, just like Jekyll and Hyde. Only those who can correctly tell right from wrong can develop strong spirits.

Isn't this exactly why Miyamoto Musashi, the famous swordsman shut himself up deep in the mountains? In his famous *Book of Five Rings*, where elements of strategy are represented by the five elements of nature—Earth, Water, Fire, Wind, and Sky—he compared the way he sought for the laws of Nature to "a fantasy drawn in a picture."

It is my interpretation that he felt that he was living in such a fantasy, where some lies or so-called fictions always exist. It is exactly the way a fantasy exists in any fight or battle. I wonder if he wanted to write about it.

His pen moves freely here and there in his book. However, when you see the pictures drawn by him, you can understand more clearly what he wanted to say in his book. Even if it is a picture, sculpture, chinaware—whatever he created—you will understand what he is like when you see things he created.

A famous great master of tea ceremony, Sen No Rikyu, was killed by his king, Hideyoshi. Rikyu's disciple, Shikibe Furuta, was also killed by the Shogun Ieyasu. However, judging by the things he created and those for the tea ceremony, we can see how great Rikyu was personally and what a respectable life he led, too.

Ninja can tell what one's life was like or one's values when they see the work one has left.

Everybody knows about unhappiness when put in a difficult situation. Such difficulties are usually of short duration. However, during the age of civil wars, this situation continued for years and years. So, if you learn how they judged things or people under such circumstances, you will be able to avert fights and troubles. If you can keep the abovementioned five precepts in mind to avoid attacks from bad people, bad family, or bad friends, it will be enough to make you a great man. When you have bad people around you, your attitude should be that God has sent them to you for a trial, that He sent them to give you a chance to prove yourself.

I have been making every effort strictly in accordance with these thousand-year-old precepts to develop a strong spirit. This is why now I have managed to keep myself on the right track in life. The old ninja story told by the late grandmaster Takamatsu is both very natural and very simple. The story, however, reflects a nature that is great, mysterious, and simple. I myself may have already become material for such stories.

I think it was Takamatsu sensei's respect for God
which made him teach in the same manner as God:
without scolding.

There are some old songs about ninjutsu: "It is your heart that
puzzles your heart . . ." or "Your rush for a win will bring you a loss
. . ." The ninja may have listened to these songs like a lullaby. Or they
may have sung them to the mountains and found the answers in the
echo. They must have listened to them not only physically but mentally.
They may have hummed the songs alone. Yes, their humming leads to
spiritual enlightenment or accomplishment of the martial art. The
melody reaches God, changes into the sound of Heaven, and takes life.
Ninja see the five precepts in the five lines of the musical score.

The Match Depends on Courage

Here, I would like you to ponder upon something. Just because one
wins matches does that mean one is strong? And is winning a good
thing? It is recorded that the great samurai Miyamoto Musashi fought
about 60 matches without losing (the perspective of) any of them. Is it
not one-sided to judge by only the wins? There must be the losing
perspective as well as the winning one. Is it not understandable that in
the world of the Yakuza there are bosses like Eigoro of Omaeda who
was respected for his dignity and never had to fight a match to prove
his strength. Thinking about this, one may wonder how many of the
legendary fighters of the world had really attained the stage of martial
master. I think there were men who never had a match but left their
mark as a master. I once received a letter from Takamatsu sensei on this
subject.

> On the eleventh, I watched you on television. It was a little different,
> but nevertheless well done. Courage is of prime importance to
> human beings. The other day Mr. A came over and I said to him, "It
> is not an overstatement to say I have taught several thousand men. Of
> all of them there is not one who has as much courage as Mr. Hat-
> sumi. He can perform any technique because of his courage." With
> my small degree of courage I have never lost one of my several tens of
> matches or any of the matches with real swords.
>
> Today, Mr. B came over and spent the night at Mr. C's house. I
> heard from Mr. C criticisms of you, your quarrel with D sensei and

other matters. I think D sensei and E sensei are both superior to you in one point or another. But you are superior to all in one point as a martial artist: your spirit. One can be called a true master only if his spirit is superior. As an old man I no longer have strength but with my superior spirit I can make the bold statement that I can beat any man of your choosing.

I parted with them saying it was the spirit that counted.

One who aims at becoming a martial master grows by courage and gains power by courage. In the fifteen years of instruction that Takamatsu sensei gave me he never scolded me once. On television when I made a mistake in my performance, he would say, "I am the one who taught you; thus it is my mistake. This is the way that it should have been done." Then he showed me the correct way to perform. I think it was Takamatsu sensei's respect for God which made him teach in the same manner as God: without scolding.

The Heritage of the Soke and the Concept of Rank

(From the Bulletin for those who aim at becoming instructors, issued in July 1982.)

My concept of the soke is always subject to change. The concept may change in accord with the flow of time or the mind and eyes of god but I do not intend to change the concept myself. I have a firm belief that I was born to guard the true will and spirit of the Kiami. At the same time, with the same guardian spirit I judge your capability and rank you accordingly. This ranking is without selfish motives. Here I would like to state what the soke is.

The history of the Togakure ryu has been made by the lives of its thirty-four inheritors. Through the mandate of God they live on within the style. Kukishin ryu had twenty-eight head inheritors, Gyokko ryu also had twenty-eight head inheritors. Koto ryu had eighteen head inheritors, Gikan ryu had fifteen, Kumogakure ryu had fourteen, Shindenfudo ryu had sixteen, Takagiyoshin ryu had seventeen, and Oshin ryu had twenty-one head inheritors.

The consciousness of these two hundred and one men is still alive within these styles. I want to be not one part of this whirlpool of consciousness but to be one with their consciousness. With this view as a constant, I am prepared to guard the dignity and responsibility of these arts. These two hundred grandmasters and I have resolved with a death-defying spirit to live according to the three principles of the

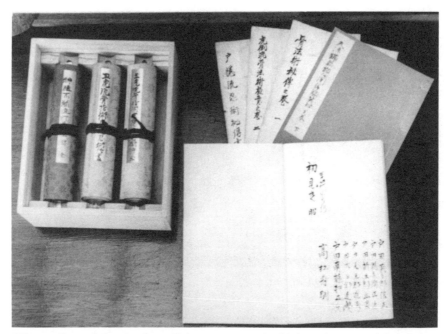

The scrolls and densho from Takamatsu sensei which make me entitled to be the soke of Togakure ryu ninjutsu.

ninja: Kaseichikusei, Banhenfukei, and Bushinwa. Putting these three as primary principles in keeping the laws of martial arts, these men have kept alive the art for eternity.

Toward the teaching I feel great gratitude; and to return the great gift I am ready to throw away my life at any time. The reason why I instruct harshly is to guard the laws of the martial arts. I have always said that a rank over the fifth grade is attained by people with god-given talent and the power that one has gained from training. No matter how strong one is or how hard one trains, one's heart only becomes darkened and darkens the heart of society when one tries to become master without these principles. These traits are the structure which maintains the laws of the art.

To see the shining power of the Soryu (inherited style) and to know it and to know oneself is to gain two hundred allies. Instructors with this wisdom will be as if surrounded by the warm gentle waves of spring and be able to fulfill the goal of life. I will repeat again that a martial master is one who has superior spirit. When reading a heroic tale, a real hero's tale can be distinguished by the superior spirit of the hero.

Parents often talk about their children affectionately, saying to

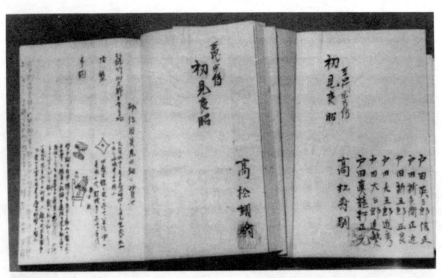

Densho of Togakure ryu ninjutsu.

others, "My sons (or daughters) were really cute and sweet in their childhood." I feel toward my students just the way parents feel toward their own children. When I think back to the time when they were still very young, I feel as happy as could be. Each of them takes a step in his own way to seek for his life. They are beginning to be independent, and they are showing their independence in various ways.

I once heard a famous, very competent manager of a professional baseball team say, "My Zen teacher, Itsugai Kajiura, said to me when I was first appointed as a manager, 'Once you were assigned to be a manager of the team by the owner Mr. Shoriki, you should do your best to fulfill your duties. To be a successful manager, you should lead the players with your back to them. If you lead them superficially, only face to face, you will never do a great job.' "

When I heard this manager tell this story, I realized that I had taught my followers face to face, and I made up my mind to change my way and lead them with my back to them.

Some people look beautiful when seen from behind. Some look strong. Sometimes women turn their backs when they are shy. You feel like smiling at such attitudes, don't you?

I have a mission to lead people with high rank. So I've got to straighten my head, turn my back to them, and live in solitude whenever necessary. As I like both listening and talking, I make it my mission to tell them old stories of the ninja, and the teachings of grandmaster Takamatsu.

I remember a story Master Takamatsu told me when I met him for the first time more than thirty years ago:

> In the first year of the Tenei era, there was a great master of Koppo; he lived calmly, peacefully—like flowers in the spring. But he was so brave that he was never afraid of fighting against one hundred thousand enemies. He could knock down a wild animal with a single blow.
>
> And he has been seeking long for a real samurai who understands and follows his spirit.

Yes, I remember clearly that he said it to me.

Cho Buren

Cho Buren lived in the Doi period of the Shin Empire (this period does not appear in the historical calendar) and came from Jyoshu. His strength and martial art techniques surpassed millions of men. His household was poor and there was hardly any furniture in the room. Sometimes he wrote poetry and drank with the other six children. I, the third child, was a gate warrior for the Chujo (magistrate) who ruled Go.

At that time, in the province of Go, there was a clever robber who could not be caught no matter how many officers were out to catch him. One night the robber sneaked into where the Chujo was sleeping and put the white blade of a knife to him. He told the Chujo to give him 100,000 ryo. The Chujo was greatly surprised and said that he could not pay that huge sum of money on a moment's notice. The official begged the robber to wait for a month. The robber replied that he would be at the temple outside the castle and to send a messenger when the Chujo had the money. Then he gave a big laugh and disappeared. The official was in shock and stood in a daze like a tree, unable to call out.

The next day, I went to see the Chujo for some business. His complexion was not good. He was so worried that he could only answer me in brief words. After a while he drew me near and began to tell me the reasons for his worries. He asked me for a plan. I replied, "The robber is skillful. I am no match for him. This is a job for my friend, Cho Buren. I think the mysterious Cho Buren will catch the robber for us."

The Chujo was greatly pleased and entrusted me with a huge sum of money to persuade Cho Buren to come to our aid. Later, Cho Buren came into the room and faced the Chujo. In addition to Buren's sleepy face and his tattered clothing, he was an inept speaker unable to put two words together. The Chujo, in his heart, was displeased and had to force himself to act properly toward Cho Buren. The Chujo turned to me and asked, "Can that man really catch the robber for us? He is a man who in the past received a scholarship in literature. Maybe I should assign him to my children and have them read various books."

Buren kept awake and strolled in the inner courtyard with his hands folded behind him. At times he would look up at the moon and recite a poem. And then suddenly, he jumped up and started to perform the martial art of Shorin.

As flexible as a phantom, he jumped as a spring and his fists like a raging storm rang throughout the inner garden's large trees and greenery. After finishing, he stood in a crane stance and for a long while called at the moon. The Chujo jumped out of the house, grabbed Cho Buren's elbow and said, "I have been stealing a look at you for a long time. I didn't realize that you are the most extraordinary fighter in this land. Master fighter, will you forgive my insolence? I would be very happy if you would save us from our worry." Buren forgave the Chujo laughingly. Then the Chujo asked if Buren could think of a plan to catch the robber.

Buren replied, "I do not know what kind of techniques the robber possesses. Would you invite the robber to your manor tomorrow? I will hide behind the screen and afterwards, I will come out and battle with the robber." The Chujo agreed and sent a messenger to call on the robber at the temple.

The robber formed a gang and came to the manor. All of the members of the gang looked confident and strong. Because of his subservient manner they trusted the Chujo. They spoke boldly and *acted as they wished. The Chujo obeyed all of their whims and urged the men to drink more. After some time had passed he retreated. Buren, in a wink's time, changed into cook's clothing and came out into the garden with a big plate in his hands. When he entered the manor, he threw the plate on the floor. The robber, greatly surprised by this, leaned against a table with one hand and flung himself into the air. He tried to escape to the roof by the ceiling beam. Cho Buren lowered his knees and in one jump grabbed onto both of the robber's feet. The robber's body split in half and the other members of the gang stood mesmerized. The legs of the table which had supported the robber were driven about six inches into the ground. This was done by the strength of Buren's hands alone.*

After all was done, the Chujo thanked Buren and gave him a thousand gold coins to show his appreciation. Buren laughed and said, "I undertook the defeat of the robbers as a simple human duty. The act was of no significance." Then, all of a sudden he was gone. Later, as he had done previously, he returned to drinking wine and composing poetry and singing with the rest of the six children. He died not once having spoken on either his martial techniques or his martial art.

10
Kamurozan

The violence man commits is self-destructive. It is the same as cannibalism in the world of animals or the slash-and-burn style of farming used by ancient man, which ends up ruining the soil and thus destroying man's source of nourishment. A ninja must be aware of the fact that violence is self-destructive, and realize the finality of the gates of Heaven and gates of Earth.

The base of the ninja beliefs lies in an obedience to the laws of nature. Abiding by nature's laws, one can climb the road to Kamurozan, the sacred mountain of universal justice. This climb makes no noise, has no scent, and leaves no shadow. These are the profound steps that we must take toward heaven.

Since I have inherited the title of soke, I live thinking the strange occurrences of nature are not strange at all and travel the road to enlightenment. I remember a saying of my master. He said that he was able to become a strong and righteous young man by training in the martial arts and mastering their mysteries; but he was not able to comprehend the real art of self-defense or become a master of martial arts—a real ninja. Until he became acquainted with the religion of the ninja, he was not able to find the blue bird that symbolizes happiness. He added that I must know the true nature of religions to be able to

The single character shinobi (to endure), drawn by Takamatsu sensei.

choose the correct one. After this conversation, I researched and analyzed various religions to find their true nature.

There are many religions in the world. As there are the killing and enlivening forms of martial arts, there are also these two types in religions. For instance, there are extremes in religious behavior: the mass suicide committed by the members of the People's Temple (Jonestown); and in olden times in Japan, a priest burned himself to death in front of the retired Emperor and nobles because of the paradise philosophy of the Jodo religion. Recently, in Japan, after the death of their leader, several female members of a religion committed suicide by burning themselves to death. There are also the tragicomedies created by extreme adherence to religious commandments: having sex be a sin or virtue, making the consumption of certain foods a sin (bulbs of plants and vegetables that are dug up from the ground, meats, etc.), fasting, forbidding the intake of liquor, making violence a sin or virtue. The lives of those who are members of these extreme religions cannot be called mentally or physically healthy. But they believe that they are happy.

My master said that today's religions are no good. Let me mention some points of Takamatsu sensei's religious thinking.

- Develop an enduring Zen spirit and understand its implications.
- Become aware of sincerity and faith (magokoro).
- Self-reflection and self-realization, then thankfulness and benevolence, are to be pursued.

Living life by being consistently aware of these realizations will lead to a righteous life and then perhaps one may live plainly in accordance with the will of God.

I think an explanation of magokoro is needed here. In Japanese, we are likely to think of this word as something like consideration, not deceiving others, serving others full-heartedly, protecting something earnestly, or something to do with correctness or good. I think that magokoro is the existence of makoto (truthfulness, sincerity, faithfulness) in the soul with a big heart surrounding it—the roots of the righteous person.

Religion is not just a thing of temples and monasteries. It is the power to develop and strengthen the weak soul and enlarge the small heart. It battles evil in the heart and reforms it into righteousness. Takamatsu sensei entered the mountains and found religion. He was enlightened to truth that could not be realized by martial arts alone.

"How difficult is life when one is not surprised by anything and laughing everyday?" drawn by Takamatsu sensei, who talks about martial arts through the world of art.

Only then did he become a master of martial arts.

Master Takamatsu said, "Let us all gain happiness by expelling grief, sorrow, and distress from our hearts. Happiness is the supreme satisfaction that this life offers. Dispel dissatisfaction and sorrow, rethink the source to find happiness."

The holy teachings of Buddha came through the Silk Road to China. In China, great enlightened priests came into being. And from one of those priests, a Japanese man received the teachings and became a priest. And then the Japanese priest taught another and then another and great wise priests developed themselves in Japan. In the same way as the growth of the community of enlightened men, the number of ninjas and martial artists has grown and now has become a community. Not only in Japan but also outside my land. The international members of our ninja community are Doron Navon, Stephen K. Hayes, Jack E. Hoban, Charles Daniel, Sveneric Bogasater, and Bud Malmstrom. In their native countries they have their own religions, but true religion has no borders. Neither does the art of the ninja.

Every country has a mountain, a sacred mountain that leads to universal justice. The sacred mountain of the ninja that I am speaking of is a vision. It is the closest place to heaven in the universe. It is always within your grasp. I want to guide you to stand on top of the sacred mountain and listen to the mysterious music of the spirits.

Ninja practicing in Kamurozan drawn by Takamatsu sensei.

Rashi and the Mendicant

Rashi, born in Kosei (a province), was a wild fellow and liked violence. He showed strength that surpassed all others and all of the merchants in the area were very subservient to Rashi. One day a crippled mendicant, who walked on his knees, came to beg at Rashi's shop. He said, "I am from Kosei but I have no income so I cannot go back there. Please, for the sake of having come from the same province, have pity on me." Being tight-fisted, Rashi tossed a one sen coin at the mendicant. The mendicant laughed scornfully, leaned his body forward, and grabbed the coin. Rashi became angry.

Counting on his strength, he flung the mendicant a huge distance. Still, the mendicant crawled nearer and Rashi flung him again. This happened three times. The mendicant finally gave up and started to turn away when he said to Rashi, "I quit. How violent and angry you are! I am a mendicant because of my disabled body. You should feel sorry for me and treat me in a kindly manner. You acted toward an invalid with violence. It cannot be considered heroic to beat me. And you have not completely beaten me. I am leaving. If anything strange happens to you, come and see me. I'll be at the rundown temple in the northern suburbs."

139

That night when Rashi moved his body to go to sleep, he could not stand the pain he felt. He undid his belt to see what was causing the pain. His underclothing was shredded into pieces. To his great surprise, he realized that the mendicant was an extraordinary man.

At dawn, he went to find the temple where the mendicant was. The beggar was sleeping on a straw mat. When he saw Rashi coming, he laughed and said, "The other day you threw me three times but you did not have enough strength." Fear and respect ran through Rashi. He bowed to the mendicant in the most respectful way (by placing his forehead on the floor). In that position he begged for the mendicant's forgiveness. The mendicant said, "Because of our similar provincial origin, I restrained my anger, but if I hadn't I would have cut off both your arms at the elbow. But your wound is not light. You must put some medication on it in order for it to heal. There's some medication on the top of the beam. Go and get it."

Rashi said apologetically that there was no way that he could do that. The mendicant jumped onto the top of the beam. The swiftness of his movement reminded Rashi of a swallow. When Rashi took the medicine that the mendicant had gotten, all of the illnesses of his body were cured.

The mendicant said in a formal manner, "Under the heavens, those who travel long distances in isolation will defend themselves with strange arts. When I was a young boy, I relied on my strength. I neglected the importance of other aspects and took my training lightly. Thus I lost my legs. Take my case as an example and avoid taking the same path." Rashi accepted this statement and took the mendicant into his home as a teacher. Until the end of his life he took care of the mendicant.

11
Ninjutsu Without
Tricks

Mysterious events are said to exist in some sort of connection with either witchcraft, the black arts, magic, religion, martial arts, hypnosis, or ninjutsu. Are the mysterious events really mysterious? Are the people who cause these events superhuman? In order to know real ninjutsu, it is an important step to clearly distinguish it from sleight of hand, witchcraft, or the black arts. What follows is an introduction to conjuring and is for the purpose of making one look at ninjutsu and martial arts from another perspective.

At the foreign correspondents club, ninjutsu is said to be a mystery of the Orient. Because of my desire to have ninjutsu looked upon as a martial art, I alternately demonstrated kenjutsu or hojutsu (danger or method tricks) and ninjutsu while explaining the difference. Of course, I explained how the trick was done as I demonstrated.

For instance, describing a trick using the Japanese sword, I said, "The Japanese sword is sharpened lengthwise, so it will not cut if I press it to my body and pull it in a certain way or if I stand on the blade." Then I put the blade on my face, tied it on with a rope and pulled the sword out. Dr. Stecker (a translator of Kawabata literature) said, "The blade must not be sharp. Let me examine it." So, I threw a

piece of bamboo up in the air and holding the sword single handed, cut the bamboo into two pieces.

When a man makes a frog fall asleep by stroking its stomach with his palm, he is praised as if he were an expert at ninjutsu or a possessor of extrasensory perception. These people are not amazing human beings but ordinary people who are good at amazing others.

In this chapter I shall explain the tricks that I performed. Please note that I am not instructing you to perform these tricks yourself, only illustrating how these tricks work.

With full force A strikes the person's forearm with his stick. The point is that he tries to strike with the portion of the stick closest to his holding hand. B tries to put his force into the part of his arm where the stick is supposed to be struck.

You can see how the physical rule works there.

Shishinjutsu involves the piercing of one's own flesh with a long needle and not bleeding or experiencing pain in the process. The most important points when performing this trick are to sterilize the needle and to choose a place which the science of anatomy has proven as the location of the least number of nerves and veins. Grab the spot as shown in the photo, aim at the precise spot, and pierce the skin in one push of the needle. At first one must pay much attention to the width of the needle; because if the needle is too wide one might bleed after the needle is pulled out thus foiling the trick. A professional of shishin-

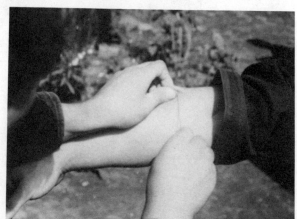

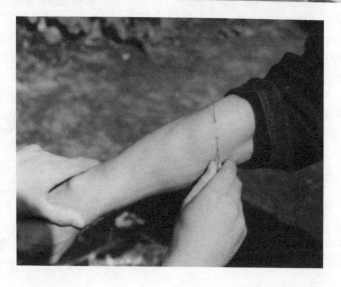

jutsu hurts when stung by a bee but he develops a callus where they insert the needle so he does not feel pain and only inserts the needle at that spot.

Make the stomach tense, free the arm of any tension, pull up the skin, and pierce the skin in one push of the needle. When pulling out the needle put pressure on the upper portion of the skin and pull it out swiftly. Then press the puncture hole with one's finger for two-and-a-half seconds which makes bleeding unlikely. The most important point when performing this trick is to avoid the vital parts of the arm or stomach. For instance, the center of the tongue has few nerves and therefore there is little pain when it is punctured. There are people who use these tricks to propogate the martial arts or demonstrate them as a result of training. When you know how these tricks are done, you can only look at them as conjurer's tricks that require no special, rigorous training, and which have no true purpose other than to amaze the simpleminded.

Do not take these tricks lightly for these tricks entail some danger.

Kairikijutsu

"Here, stand on my right hand and hold on tight to my waist," says the performer.

Then the full weight of a grown man is held by one hand of this ultra-strong man!! But when I explain the trick it becomes evident that this is not such an amazing feat. The key lies in the words "Hold on tight to my waist . . . ." At that moment the performer stands up with

the man's weight on his waist. Using this method, one can hold a desk by the mouth with the leg of the desk on his waist, then concentrating all of one's strength on the waist, a woman can dance on the table.

A man stands up and says, "Lift me up." The other man lightly lifts him. Then the first man says, "Lift me up again." This time it is as if the first man has gained weight; the challenged man cannot lift him. This is fudojutsu (immobility trick). This is actually done by shifting the location of the center of gravity of his weight. All one has to do when one wants to be lifted is to lean forward and put both arms forward.

Another trick is done with an extremely strong man putting his arms forward in front of his chest and holding one end of a stick with both of his hands. The performer holds the other end of the stick with only his right hand. The two begin a pushing contest. At this time the performer lowers the position of his waist and pushes the stick diagonally upwards. The strong man will lose this contest to a small man using only one arm. This is an application of the science of dynamics, not magic. One may see another application in the way sumo wrestlers lower their waists, and attack with their hands in upward movements.

Next is a trick where a performer holding a six-foot stick with his little finger pushes back an opponent who is pushing the other end with all of his might. The performer has the tip of the stick on his little finger and the opponent pushes the stick from the other end with both his hands on the stick. The bone of the finger does not break, but in fact the single digit pushes back the opponent. This is done with a little gimmick. The stick which appears to be on the little finger alone is actually on the second portion of the middle finger. This is the portion that the performer is pushing with.

The other tricks of kairikijutsu involve breaking ropes, bending metal bars, breaking chains, and actions to be taken when choked. Some of the actions to take when choked involve withstanding the pressure by the strength of one's jaw, jaw tendon, and shoulder.

Nawanuke and Tejyonukejutsu

A ninja is said to be able to slip through ropes by dislocating his joints. There are people who say that since it is inappropriate for martial arts performers to maintain a state where the joints can be dislocated when fighting, performers hardly ever use this.

One can easily slip through ropes by using the technique illustrated in the photographs. But make sure to choose the material carefully. It is easier to slip through if tied tightly by a thick rope than a thin rope.

First, open your tied hands and use the width of your hand to loosen the knot, then slip through thumb first.

Repeated dislocation of the wrist, elbow, or shoulder joints is disadvantageous to the martial artist but there are times when the artist may find this method useful. There are those who say that a ninja hides a knife up his neckband to cut the rope, but such an action would make the opponent cautious. There are ways of having someone discharge an arrow with the knife or key or using an animal to bring the articles. Also one can use hensojutsu (the art of deception) to slip through the rope.

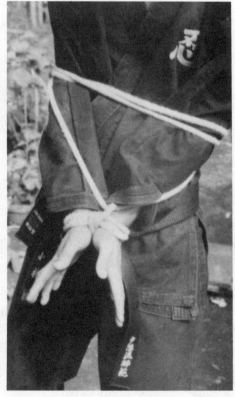

There was an artist in America who could slip through any kind of handcuffs but he never exposed his method. After his death, there was much research into his method but it was finally decided that he had extraordinary wrist joints. It is easy to slip through handcuffs but considering the antisocial uses that the methods can be used for they will not be presented here.

Dobutsushidojutsu

A snake can be immobilized by holding it with the left hand and squeezing it three times with the right. If it is still moving, press the vital part.

When the legendary swordsman Miyamoto Musashi was having a meal at a tea house, palanquin bearers tried to lead him into a duel. Musashi sat silently and caught live flies, which were annoying his meal, with his chopsticks. Seeing this the bearers ran away in fear. This trick is accomplished by seizing the flies at the moment when they are rubbing their hind and forelegs together while deciding to fly or not;

> When a man makes a frog fall asleep by stroking its stomach with his palm, he is praised as if he were an expert at ninjutsu or a possessor of extrasensory perception. These people are not amazing human beings but ordinary people who are good at amazing others.

or when they are concentrating wholly on the food.

To seize a fish, hold it up gently upside down pressing its eyes. An expert at catching koi (carp) uses this method. Utilize this method to catch your koi (love). Hah!

There is a man in Yamato who claims to have won a battle with a bear. When he was attacked, he forgot his fear in his panic, and charged into the bear sticking his hand in the bear's mouth and twisting its tongue off. The bear was killed.

In China, Takamatsu sensei and his Chinese friend were walking down a country road when they were attacked by several Chinese dogs. The largest dog, as big as a Saint Bernard, came charging at sensei. With its fangs out and its forelegs on sensei's shoulders, the animal was ready to sink his fangs into sensei. At that moment, sensei stood fearlessly still and peered at the dog with his left eye. When sensei was studying the arts of the ninja from the master Toda Shinryu, he was taught that even the fiercest animal will not attack if one stood suddenly still. At the moment when the dog stopped growling, his right fist struck the dog on the nose. The dog fell defeated and the other dogs darted off in fear. The art of immobilizing an animal must be used after having carefully observed the behavior of the animal.

Homo sapiens is also an animal. Let me introduce you to a few tricks that street showmen often use. The tricks are called fudokanashi-barinojutsu. The number of people do not matter. Make them bend their elbows at ninety-degrees, put their arms in front of their bodies and make them turn their arms in a circular motion. Then unexpectedly kiai (yell). Their arms will freeze in position. Next, take the arms still bent at ninety degrees and carefully turn them to the back and hold them there. In this way, the arms can maintain this folded position.

The performer makes a person lie down on the floor face up. He tells the person to stick out his stomach, thus bending the body in a bow-

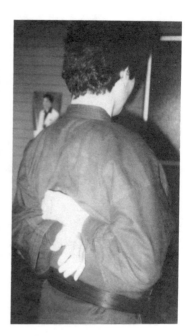

like fashion or like a round bridge. This makes it appear as though the body were really stiffened. Then place his upper torso and legs onto a chair. In this position, one or two lightweight persons can sit on his stomach without the person's body collapsing under the pressure. Even if an especially large rock were placed on the person's stomach and smashed with an iron hammer, he would be fine. There are performers where a person in this position has a heavy wooden bowl containing sticky rice placed on his stomach and then the rice is pounded with a wooden hammer into rice cake. Another is to place a daikon (long white radish) on the person's stomach and halve it with a sword.

Chochufudojutsu

There is a trick that performers use to make a passer-by unable to walk by giving a kiai. The key is to yell just when he is about to raise his leg to take another step.

Knowing such natural phenomena can be helpful in martial arts.

A dominoes effect can be created with many people by making them stand in an unstable stance. The more participants the more unstable the stance must be for the trick to succeed. When one person loses his balance, another will follow suit and one after another they will all fall down. With expert oratory, make them concentrate fully on your words and use your words to affect their spirit strings to force them down. All these strength tricks are done by using the balance of the person to make them fall and to make their body seem heavy or light.

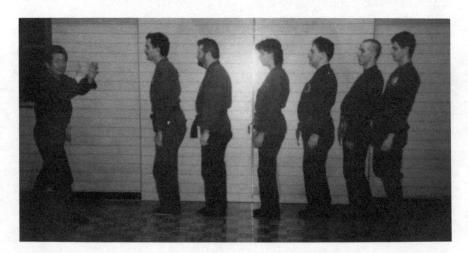

Standing on Nails or Broken Glass

Place ten or so sheets of metal with nails sticking up on them one after the other and stand on top of them barefoot. You should not experience pain because the weight of your body is divided onto all the nails that you are standing on. With this principle the more closely the nails are placed the less pain one experiences.

Escalating the use of this principle, there are many performances that have been developed. Lying on a pile of nails a man may have another stand on top of him, have something heavy placed on him, have a big rock placed on his stomach and shattered with a metal hammer (in the same way as mentioned previously), or have a wooden plaque placed on top of him and then have a car drive over him.

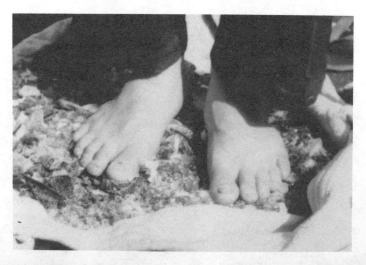

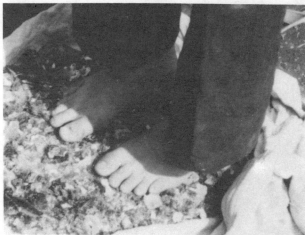

One will not be hurt when standing on top of shattered glass if there is a large pile of the glass. This is because the weight of one's body is evenly distributed onto all the pieces under one's feet. Perform this trick only when there is a large pile of glass. This is using the same principle as when one stands on or lies on countless numbers of nails. There will no pain for the weight of the body is distributed on hundreds of nails.

The skin at the bottom of the feet is the thickest on the human body. When getting off the pile of glass, make sure to brush off the pieces of glass. A single piece of glass will easily rupture the skin.

Tricks Using the Japanese Sword

As mentioned previously a Japanese sword cuts lengthwise. Therefore, it will not cut even when a person stands on it if he knows how to move on and off. People who cut long radishes on top of a person's stomach and squeeze the sword with their bare hands know the characteristics of the sword. When I was lecturing to the Prince about the art of the ninja, one of the students from Gakushu In said that the sword I was using must not be able to cut. He touched the blade with his finger tip and cut himself. As this example proves, for persons who do not know the characteristics of the sword, tricks with the blade can be hazardous. It should be mentioned that the sword tricks cannot be done with small swords, razor blades, or kitchen knives because they all cut differently.

Likewise, knowledge of the Japanese sword characteristics, the feel of the cut, should be studied as reference for use in holding the blade. Since blades should be treated as living tools and because of the great chance of injuries, these and other blade tricks should be studied under an experienced master and never without guidance.

Iai jutsu

With such specious statements as "I am a master of the quick draw,' some performers cut chopsticks with paper or break a bamboo hanging from paper in two. These tricks have nothing to do with true iai jutsu but are the products of dynamics, inertia, or sleight of hand.

For example, there is a trick where the performer gives a yell and cuts through a bundle of ten or so chopsticks held by a member of the audience with only one chopstick. As can be seen in the photos, the sticks were not cut with the single chopstick but with a hand blade.

There was a man who performed such tricks on television claiming to be a master of iai jutsu. As time passed, he disappeared from the screen. The other day this man gave me a call. Then a man who used to appear on television with him said to me, "Sensei, wasn't there a call from a man claiming to be a ninja, just a while ago? Please be aware of him because he is a terrible con artist!"

Originally, ninjutsu was not to be performed in front of an audience. For over a thousand years the people of my school have kept ninjutsu a secret. Perhaps, this secrecy made it possible for me to be born. I sometimes reconsider the vital importance of this secrecy.

The tricks that I have introduced are also called danger tricks or method tricks. These tricks are performed by magicians, street performers, religious preachers, and supposed ninjas as proof of mastery in martial arts. They are not performed for entertainment by real masters, experts, or enlightened persons and are not proof of mastery. In my view, they are nothing to be awed about. These tricks are against the fundamental characteristics of ninjutsu. Please keep this in mind. If you wish to perform these only as tricks, you should seek out an instructor to help you. They are tricks which require intelligence rather than training or martial arts skill.

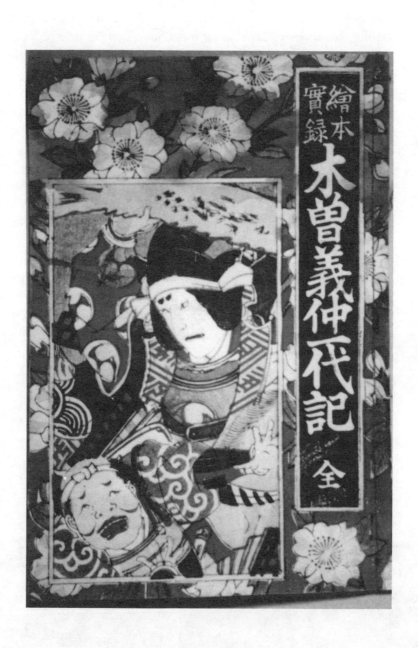

12
The Child's Mind

When I was visiting the U.S. one time, I was delighted at someone calling me "cute boy." To me, it was a very refreshing and pleasant moment. Children have amazing senses of vision and hearing and are even capable of making keen judgments sometimes. In this chapter, I would like to introduce the roots of the ninja spirit by bringing out some of the underlying significance of the child's mind.

When we speak about ninjutsu, we cannot give a thorough explanation just by focusing on the aspects of religion and the martial arts alone. More importantly, it cannot be understood if you are only to rely on your own senses of the adult world. We often tend to lose sight of things that are much more important because of this. So, let's try to search for new dimensions of light and sound through the eyes and ears of a child.

First, let's look at the *Kojiki*, a record of ancient matters written in 712 A.D. It contributes a great deal to our understandings of the Japanese history and mythology.

There were sibling dieties named Ama terasu oho mi kami (The Heaven–Shining–Great–August–Diety) and Susa no wo no mikoto (The Brave-Swift-Impetuous-Male-Augustness). Susa no wo no mikoto was a very rowdy god and was always up to some evil acts. One day, as Ama terasu oho mi kami sat in her sacred weaving-hall, he broke a hole in the top of the hall and threw a heavenly horse skin into it. Thereupon, Ama terasu oho mi kami closed the door of the heavenly Rock-Dwelling and retired to admonish him. Deity of the sun that she was, the whole world was obscured and darkened.

A quarrel between a sister and a brother is depicted here, and we can regard these two deities as a sister state and a brother state as well. Metaphorically speaking, the act of throwing the horse skin can be interpreted as an act of ridicule or condemnation. Despite such an insult, however, the great sun goddess of magnanimous mind never displays her anger but conceals herself behind the heavenly Rock-Dwelling instead. This very act, involving stoicism and endurance, is what the ninja spirit stems from.

A child playing with a covered bamboo sword. A child has a genius for finding happiness in any small thing. Grown-ups are forgetful of the true happiness in small things.

The reign of the rowdy god cannot last long. Owing to this, the Deities assembled in a divine assembly and planned many contrivances, including bird-singing and dancing. The bird-singing here can be taken as a symbol for the rising sun. Astonished by the laughing and singing voices of the festival outside, the great sun goddess opened the door slightly to see what was happening there. Then Ta jikara wo no kami (The Heavenly-Hand-Strength-Male-Deity), who was standing hidden, waiting for this moment, quickly pulled the door wide open and the great sun goddess came forth, making the whole world happy and light again.

Ta jikara wo no kami was a man of the great strength as you can see here, but we can also say that he opened the door with the spirit of the martial arts—that is, he sincerely related to the heart of the great sun goddess and succeeded in opening her closed mind with his spiritual power. This book contains a number of such teachings including the stupidity of a man who, at times, turns his kinship love into complete hatred.

Injiuchi—mock fighting with stone missiles.

Injiuchi gave birth to shuriken or blade throwing.

The first emperor in Japan was the Emperor Jinmu. When he founded the country, he tried to avoid unnecessary wars and established peace in the whole country with love and mercy. As the "Japanese mind" is called yamato damashii (literally it means a big, united spirit), it is grounded in that great awareness for protecting peace, and I would like to convey to you that this spirit still continues to live in all of us today.

It is from such spirits that we discover various ways of life. And there were many who expressed their human experiences in different forms, be it a poem or literature. Those great masterworks they left still have a power to touch our hearts. Takamatsu sensei once said to me, "Martial artists are not everything. You should have a get-together with all the good people around you, young and old. Protect those people so they can live a happy life. This is also the spirit of the martial arts, my boy." Now, not only can I hear his voice, but I can actually see it and relate to it.

I am very fond of Kobayashi Issa, a haiku poet who saw the world through the eyes of a child. I would like to introduce some of his haiku poems and give my comments on each one. Let's start with one of the most famous ones of all:

> Never give up, Skinny Frog!
> I, Issa, will always be on your side.

This is about some male frogs competing against each other for one female frog to mate with. The weak skinny frog is pushed away by the bigger ones, but he tries again and again. I feel a similar sense of the mysteries of the martial arts in this poem—the spiritual strength is all you need!

> Don't swat it! The fly is wringing his hands . . .
> he's wringing his feet.

When you gaze at a fly wringing its hands and feet, it looks as if he is begging us not to kill the poor thing. This poem suggests to me that it is wrong to kill such a vulnerable fly. The master of Ninja never wantonly kills.

> The day has passed again,
> while I have been made light of by
> the fleas and flies.

Besides the straightforward meaning of this poem, I can also see the reflection of the ninja's spirit in this one. If you replace fleas and flies with people, it becomes more explicit: "The day has passed again while I have been made light of by vain people." However, this should not be regarded as a depressing thought. Rather, this poem provides a more profound meaning: that a person who always has to put others down is wasting his day and life and he, who does not realize that, deserves our pity.

> Don't jump, Flea!
> That is the Kakuta River
> in front of you.

This one can be interpreted as a lesson for hasty acts. As said in the proverb, "Haste makes waste." If you don't control your own acts, you may fall into the River of Sanzu, the river flowing through hell. You may drown in the infernal river if you go against nature and lose yourself in greed for fame and wealth.

> You, Baby sparrow!
> Hop and skip aside . . .
> because the horse is passing by.

The baby sparrow is playing in the middle of the road and he is not aware of the horse. As the horse comes closer, Issa kindly gives the baby sparrow warning to step aside. However, if you consider the baby sparrow as a beginner in martial arts, you will realize that the poem applies to the world of the martial arts as well. There are many dangers in the world of martial arts if you don't know enough about it. Therefore, you have to learn to own a quick eye for dangers in order to master the secrets of the art.

> Come along with me, orphan sparrows.
> Let's play together.

This poem should be the continuation of the last one. For those enthusiastic beginners who can find no true teacher, it is a senior who is to be their friend and teacher.

Basho is another famous haiku poet, a man who loved travelling. nature, and people. He brought the art of haiku to its height by adding touches of sabi (elegant simplicity), wabi (taste for the simple and

Hide and seek leads to Do ton or Seki ton jutsu (earth or stone concealment techniques)

quiet), shiori (gentleness), hosomi (fineness), and karumi (lightness) to his haiku poetry. Indeed, he was much aware of little changes in Mother Nature, and captured the beauty of its eternal power and harmony in his words. No one can deny that he was one of the greatest poets, but we can also say that he was a searcher and a philosopher as well.

Yosano Buson, one of Basho's students, was the one who gave diversity to haiku and went far beyond the formality of it. As some regard him as a playful poet who took pleasure in beauty, Buson's poetry has no element of coercion or violence. And when you look at his artworks or haiku, you cannot but feel his warm sense of intimacy and nostalgia. The martial arts I am questing for and the world of haiku can meet each other in such a line.

During the Taisho and the beginning of the Showa period, Noguchi Ujo, a poet, expressed the child's mind explicitly in his works. His poems, too, do not appear to show any aggressive nature, but the profound messages carried consistently in his poems are powerful and convincing. Ujo's poems and the music of Nakayama Shimpei produced many children's song. For some reason, these songs have a magical power to make all adults feel ease and grace.

Ninjutsu expands a children's romantic world. As time changes, so does the child's world. The picture is the hero of "Ninja Animaru," a comic magazine serial currently popular in Japan.

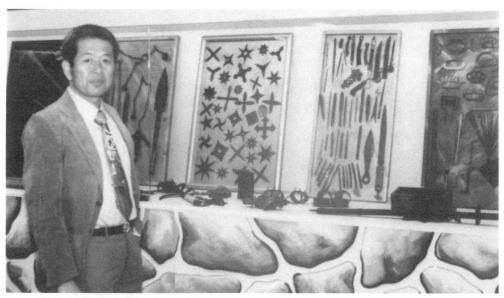

Various ninja tools the author possesses.

Author giving autographs.

Mr. Kamiya Minoru, the comic artist of "Ninja Animaru."

Author and Mr. Kamiya, talking about the ninja.

True strength and greatness often come from such little things around you, and if you cannot find the value in them, you no longer should be called a martial artist. Sound body and mind make the world as one. They can coexist because they are universal. When body and mind are rejuvenated, one can discover the highest reach of art: simplicity. The poems of Ujo and the music of Nakayama Shimpei can relate to people all around the world.

The style of these two men's works can even share similarities with the folk songs of Scotland. The melodies of the Scottish folk songs, such as "Bell-Flower," "Annie-Laurie," and "Greensleeves," create deep harmony with the heart of Japanese children's songs. As some of you may already know, what I would like to point out here is that the perception, innocence, and ideas of a child as well as memories of one's childhood all serve the purpose of the martial arts and ninjutsu.

In ninjutsu, there is a technique called Yoton no jutsu which incorporates the child's mind. Yoton no jutsu is thought by many people to be a technique using a child as one of the tools. However, it is a technique geared to the child's mind instead of using a real child, and as you can see from what I have been writing, it does not work effectively without skillful flexibility of mind. Children are, or should be, regarded as the treasures of the nation. In a Kurdistan proverb, they say, "Evil has no power over a family blessed with many children."

For the readers of my book, I would like to tell you that I will always be watching over you. Be tolerant of the criticism of others. It's not so difficult if you take them just as those of a child. I should be happy if I could help you to understand the spirit of the ninja and the essence of their techniques through this book.

Brief History of the Ninja Taken from the Densho Scrolls

- Ninja rendered distinguished services in restoring peace to the province known as Yamato (present-day Osaka district) for Emperor Jinmu, and also in suppressing barbarians—subsequently known as the Ainu.
- Ninja raised an army in loyalty to the Southern Court of Yoshino (1331–33 A.D.). They joined the armies of Nawa, Kusunoki, Kitabatake (1334–35 A.D.).
- Ninja put the Ashikaga Army into confusion (1487-88 A.D.).
- They joined the army of Sekita and chased the large army of Hosokawa Takakuni under the Ashikaga shogun's command (1504–20).
- In those days, the ninja had no specific schools like Koga or Iga ryu, and were just distinguished by the name of the places where they lived. Ninja living in both Koga and Iga provinces were royalists. However, when Ashikaga Yoshitane dispatched his troops to the Omi district to subdue Ashikaga Yoshizumi, Koga ninja took sides with Yoshitane while the Iga ninja would not, which caused discord between ninja of Koga and Iga.
- Iga ninja cooperated with the Royalists army (1854–59), and joined a squad of the court patrolmen and troubled the

Shinsengumi or bodyguard party of the Tokugawa government organized in the closing days of the shogunate.

- In 1863, some ninja joined the Tenchugumi or a group of extremists headed by Yoshimura Torataro, Fujimoto Tesseki, and others who tried to overthrow the Tokugawa shogunate. They rose in arms to no effect and many of them were killed.
- Ninja distinguished themselves in the field of battle against the Tokugawa government. In the battle of Toba Fushimi, which was fought between the Royalists and the loyalists of the Tokugawa shogunate just after the decree of the Restoration of Royal Rule in 1886, ninja joined the Royalist party, distinguishing themselves in it.

Record of the Origin of Togakure Ryu

The Togakure ryu school of ninjutsu dates back to Togakure Daisuke in the period of Oho (1161–62). He received his training in ninjutsu from Kagakure Doshi. One July during the Hogen period (1156–59), Shima Kosanta Minamoto no Kanesada, aged 16, and a powerful clan in the Ise province, joined the army of Minamoto Yoshinaka and fought with three thousand horsemen of the Fujiwara Hidehira army. Lying fallen in the battlefield seriously injured, Shima was saved by Kagakure Doshi and they fled into the mountains of Iga. It is said that he received his training in martial arts as well as ninjutsu from Kagakure Doshi. In later years he was celebrated as the second grand-master of the Togakure ryu ninjutsu.

Legend has it that there was a ninja named Ikai who lived under the So regime of Korai (present-day Korea) from the late tenth to early eleventh centuries. In the first year of the Kouyu era he fought a losing battle against King Jinso together with the armies of Kittan and Ka. Then he fled to Japan, landing at Ise and lived in a cave in Iga province. It was recorded that Ikai was a military commander proficient in hicho kakuregata (concealment techniques based on hicho jutsu). And it is said that he could jump many meters high with a yell. Apparently, Ikai was the first to introduce ninjutsu to Japan.

There is another candidate for founder, however, in the Jiryaku period (1065-68). Fujiwara Chikado entrenched himself in a cavern at Mt. Takao by Taneo village because the court didn't grant him the rank he had requested. This cave is said to have been built by Ikai when he had fled from Korea a few years before.

The record says that there have been seventy-three schools of ninjutsu throughout its history. Some of the main schools are as follows: Negishi ryu, Shirai ryu, Shinto ryu, and Hakuun ryu, from which such schools as Togakure ryu, Koushu ryu, Kishu ryu, Minamoto ryu, Genjitu ryu, Ryumon ryu, Tenton happo ryu, and Goton juppo ryu are said to have been derived.

Iga ryu and Koga ryu survived long enough to gain such a high reputation that they were welcomed by the Tokugawa government.

Hakuun ryu was initiated by Garyu doji and later completed by the time of Hakuun doji. It is said that Hakuun ryu featured the flexible usage of four demons: shadow demon, fire demon, earth demon, and wind demon. During the Oho period approximately a hundred years after the Jiryaku era, Kagakure doji, who was a disciple of Hakuun doji, imparted training in ninjitsu to Togakure Daisuke, who in turn

took care of Shima Kosanta. As mentioned above, there is a record that in those days quite a few survivors of the Kiso Yoshinaka's army fled into the mountains of Iga province. Later on during the Engen (1336–39) and Shohei (1346–69) eras, a number of stragglers from both the South and the North Courts are said to have sneaked into the mountains of Iga and Koga provinces. Some say that this fact marks the origin of various schools of the ninja including Iga and Koga ryu.

According to the records of Koga ninjutsu, during the Tenkyo era (938–46), Mochizuki Saburo Kaneie, the third son of Suwa Saemon

Minamoto Shigeyori, governor of the Shinano province, distinguished himself in war against the Taira no Masakado's revolt and was promoted to the governor of the Koga gun, southeast of the Omi province. He changed his name from Mochizuki Saburo Kaneie to Koga Oumi no kami Kaneie. His son, named Oumi no kami Iechika, had literary and military accomplishments and it is said that he learned genjutsu from a Buddhist monk called Tatsumaki Hoshi, a master of genjutsu, who lived in Koga province. Some insist that this originated the Koga ryu of ninjutsu.

The successors of the Koga school are Ienari, Iesada, Ienaga, Iekiyo, Iekuni, Ietoo, Ieyoshi, and Yoshiyasu. Of the offspring, four other families—the Mochizuki, the Ugai, the Naiki, and the Akutagawa—

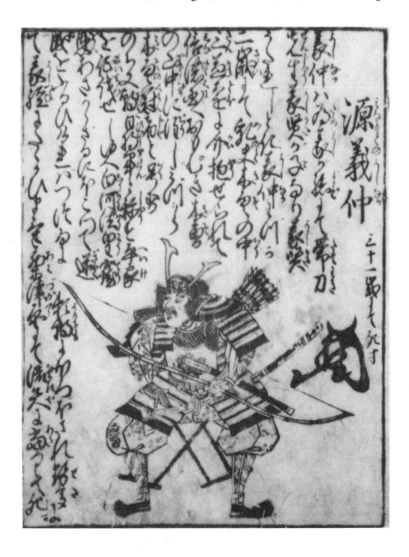

became the main stocks of the Koga lineage. In the Hotoku era (1449-51), five successors, Koga Saburo, Mochizuki Goro, Ugai Ryuhoshi, Naiki Fujibe, and Akutagawa Kazuma were recorded. During the Bunmei era (1469-86), Koga Saburo II, Mochizuki Yajiro, Ukai Chiaki, Naiki Gohei, and Akutagawa Tenpei spearheaded the Sasaki army to defeat the troops of Ashikaga Yoshihisa. In addition to these five families, the groups of the remnant troops of the South and North courts constituted 53 families of the Koga lineage. Of these, eight families, the Koga, Mochizuki, Ugai, Naiki, Akutagawa, Ueno Ban, and Nagano rose to prominence and were called the Strong Eight. In addition, Hiryugumi and Hakuryugumi also produced masters of ninpo.

Here are brief lists of the star ninja of the ninjutsu families:
Hiryugumi: Yamanaka Juro, Saga Echizen no kami, Miyajima Gyubunosuke, Kuraji Ukonnosuke, and Heishi Mondonosuke.

- Hakuryugumi: Katuragi Tango no kami, Sugitani Yotoji, Kiyama Shikanosuke, Mochizuki Izumo no kami, Wada Iga no kami, Hari Izumi no kami, Oki Ukontaro, Akutagawa Sakyomaru, and Uda Tonai.
- Tairagumi: Torii Heinai, Sugiyama Hachiro, Hattori Fujitaro, Okawara Gennai, Okubo Gennai, Saji Kochi no kami, and Takamine Kurando.
- Bangumi: Ohara Genzaburo, Ban Sakyonosuke, Makimura Umanosuke, Ueno Shuzennosho, Taki Kantaro, Noda Goro, Iwane Nagatonokami, and Kokawa Bunnai.
- Fujiwaragumi: Ugai Genpachiro, Ogawa Magojuro, Yamagami Toshichiro, Hatta Kansuke, Tongu Shikinosuke, Kamiyama Shinpachiro, Iwamuro Daigakunosuke, Nakayama Minbunojo, Takayama Gentazaemon, Ikeda Shouemon, Nagano Gyobunojo, Naiki Iganokami, Ono Miyauchinoshosuke, and Shinjo Etsunokami.
- Tataragumi: Aoki Chikugonokami, Koizumi Geki, Natsumi Daigaku, Tarao Shirobe, and Tanba Migumo Shinkuraudo.
- Sugawaragumi: Minobe Genkichi, and Akimoto Kozunosuke Masahide.
- Koremunegumi: Shinpo Heinai, Takamatsu Isenokami, Aiba Kawachinokami, and Takano Bigonokami.
- Kawachi Shitengugumi: Shinno Kuranosuke, Tatsumi Jiro, and Honda Chikuzennokami.
- Tachibana Hachitengugumi: Kounishi Tomogo, Kido Yamatonokuni, Endo Mushanosuke, and Sekiguchi Genjuro.

The second grandmaster of the Koga ryu had three children, who were called Tenryu Koga, Chiryu Koga, and Aranami Koga, respectively.

According to the records of the Iga ryu, Iga Heinaibe Yasukiyo who received training from Gamondouji took sides with Minamoto no Yoritomo, the founder of the Kamakura government. He was granted the land of Iga Hattori where he built Iga castle. This is the origin of the Iga school of ninjutsu.

The first grandmaster was Gamondouji in the Jiryaku period (1065-68).

The second grandmaster was Garyudouji in the Shouho period (1074-76).

The third grandmaster was Unryudouji in the same period.

Tozawa Hakunsai, in the Heiji period (1159); Iga Heinaibe Yasukiyo, in the Eicho period (1096); Ise Saburo Yoshimori in the Heiji
period (1159); Togakure Daisuke, in the Shogen period (1207-10);
Kumogakure Gen-an, in the Kencho period (1249-55); Tozawa Seiun,
in the Shouou period (1288-92); Tozawanyudo Gen-eisai, in the
Kenmu period (1334-35); Hachimon Hyouun, in the Kouryaku period (1379-80); Kuryuzu Hakuun, in the Oiei period (1394-1427);
Tozawa Ryutaro, in the Chokyo period (1487-88); Momochi Sandayu
I, in the Tenmon period (1532-54); Momochi Sandayu II, in the
Tensho period (1573-91); Iga Heinai Saemon no jo Ienaga (the
twelfth generation from Heinaibe Yasukiyo), in the Tenmon period
(1532-54); his eldest son, Kamihattori Heitaro Koreyu; the second
son, Nakahattori Heijiro Yasuyori; the third son, Shimohattori Heijuro
Yasunori.

In the ninth year of the Eiroku era (1558-69), Oda Nobunaga
attacked the Iga family because they didn't obey his orders. The three
Hattori families were completely defeated and 80 survivors fled for
refuge. The survivors of the Kamihattori fled to Nagaoka in the Echigo
province; those of the Shimohattori found protection from the
Tokugawa family in the Mikawa province or the Ochi family in Taka-
tori, Yamato; those of the Nakahattori fled deep in the mountains of
Takano, Kishu. In the Eiroku period (1558-69) Hattori Hanzo and
Hattori Masanari of the Kamihattori family swore allegiance to Tokugawa Ieyasu.

The following are star ninjas of the Hattori family: Hattori Gensuke,
Hattori Denjiro, Hattori Denemon, Hattori Magohei, Hattori Naizo,
Hattori Shinkuro, Hattori Shichikuro, Hattori Jinroku, Yamaoka
Sobei, Yamaoka Suketaro, Tsuge Sannojo, Tsuge Ichinosuke, Tsuge
Jintaro, Yamaguchi Jinsuke, Fukunokami Teisainyudo, Yamanaka Ka-
kubei, Hanchi Hansuke, Naruto Iga, Akimoto Kassai, Sera Genroku,
Otsuka Bansaku, and Yamanouchi Keitaro.

In the Tensho period (1573-91) the Ryugu village under the governor Kitabatake Tomonori at Uda Sanbonmatsu in Yamato province was
founded. The leading figures were as follows: Momochi Tanbayasu-
mitsu or lord of the Ryugu castle, Momochi Tarozaemon. The lords of
the castle of Ueno Shokudai, Mie, were Momochi Sandayu or lord of
the castle of Ueno Shokudai in the Mie province, Momochi Jindayu
Yasutatsu, Momochi Chuzaburo Yasumasa, Momochi Sannojo, Nom-
ura Oidayu, Shindo Kotaro, Tateoka Dojun, Shimotuge Kizaru, Ueno
Suke, Yamada Hachiemon, Kanbe Konami, Otowa Joto, Suzuki Tendo,

Otsuka Bansaku, Nagano Takemon, Fujimoto Genki, Tada Shintaro, Koyama Tenzen, Sugimoto Sarunosuke, Kojima Ryuun, Namikawa Kinzo, and Segawa Shinnosuke.

The forty-five families of the Iga ryu are as follows: Tozawa, Fujiwara, Minamoto, Taira, Momochi, Hattori, Izumo, Okuni, Tsutsumi, Arima, Hata, Mizuhara, Shima, Togakure, Ise, Sakagami, Narita, Oda, Mori, Abe, Ueno, Otsuka, Ibuki, Kaneko, Kotani, Shindo, Iida, Kataoka, Kanbe, Sawada, Kimata, Toyata, Toda, Suzuki, Kashiwabara, Fukii, Iga, Kuriyama, Kimura, Kazama, Sugino, Hisahara, Ishitani, Hanbe, and Ooyama.

Index